The
MANTLE
of the
FATHER'S HEART

The MANTLE *of the* FATHER'S HEART

It's Your Mantle!

DR. BENEDITA MONTEIRO GOMES

XULON PRESS

Xulon Press
2301 Lucien Way #415
Maitland, FL 32751
407.339.4217
www.xulonpress.com

Unless otherwise indicated, Scripture quotations taken from the King James Version (KJV) – *public domain*.

Printed in the United States of America.

Paperback ISBN-13: 978-1-6628-0019-1
Hardcover ISBN-13: 978-1-6628-0020-7
eBook ISBN-13: 978-1-6628-0021-4

Table of Contents

Dedication

This book is dedicated to my intelligent, amazing and beloved sister Maria Alina Gomes Monteiro Connolly for her support and words of encouragement throughout my life such as *"There is nothing that you do in this lifetime that will ever surprise me."* And *"If Dita were rich, the whole family would benefit because of her giving heart."* These are some of her inspirational words that have helped me stay positive. She has always shown love and wisdom in her delivery. Mana, indeed, you are the best sister ever, and I appreciate and love you very much! Uum kreb tcheu e Deus bençuob, sempre!

Acknowledgment

I wish to acknowledge my deepest gratitude and appreciation for my beautiful, intelligent and amazing niece Dives Alice Lopes for her support in editing this book. I also wish to acknowledge my dear friend Pastor Dr. Doretha Cale for capturing the vision of the Mantle of the Father's Heart and painting the perfect book cover.

First Things First
You do not have this book in your hands by accident. The Father is calling you to Him; however, for you to fully benefit from this book, you must be born again and filled with His Holy Spirit. Thus, the reason for the following prayers. *"For God so loved the world, that he gave his only begotten Son, that whosoever believeth in him should not perish, but have everlasting life" (John 3:16 KJV).*

Prayer for the Reader
Salvation Prayer
Lord Jesus,
I believe in my heart, and I confess with my mouth that you came and died for my sins. I ask you to forgive me of all my sins and to come into my life and to become my Lord and Savior. Thank you, Jesus, for forgiving me of all my sins and for setting me free from all unrighteousness. *"That if thou shalt confess with thy mouth the Lord Jesus, and shalt believe in thine heart that God hath raised him from the dead, thou shalt be saved. For with the heart, man believeth*

unto righteousness; and with the mouth, confession is made unto salvation" (Rom 10:9-10 KJV).

Holy Spirit Baptism Prayer

Lord Jesus,

I believe you and your Word. I repent of all my sins, and I ask you to forgive me.

Lord, I know that according to your Word, Jesus, you have forgiven me, and you remember my sins no more. Thank you for forgiving me. Lord, I forgive myself as well. Lord Jesus, thank you for your precious Holy Spirit. Holy Spirit, I welcome you in my life. I honor you with my life, and I ask you to become my teacher, my counselor, my comforter, my protector, my everything. Holy Spirit, thank you for coming into my life and being my teacher, my counselor, my comforter, my protector, my everything. Now, open your mouth in faith, and let the Holy Spirit feel your mouth. You will feel a tingling in your tongue or mouth, and sometimes your jaws will feel a bit heavy. Don't worry; it is the Holy Spirit. He will speak through you if you just believe and humble yourself before Him. *"Then Peter said unto them, Repent, and be baptized every one of you in the name of Jesus Christ for the remission of sins, and ye shall receive the gift of the Holy Ghost. For the promise is unto you, and to your children, and to all that are afar off, even as many as the Lord our God shall call" (Acts. 2:38-39 KJV).*

Dear Heavenly Father,

I come to you right now boldly in the name of Jesus. Father, I come covered in the precious blood of your Son, Jesus Christ. I come with confidence in the blood sacrifice of Jesus at the Cross of Calvary. I know you hear me because your ears are always attentive to your Son's blood.

Mercy Seat,
Speak on my behalf and that of the readers of this book and their loved ones. Help us to grasp the power in the authority of the mantle of Jesus Christ, our Lord and Savior. Help us to apply the mantle to our daily lives so that we may walk in the power of the overflow of Christ Jesus' resurrection. All this I ask and receive in Jesus' name, and I receive it all for Jesus' glory. Amen!

Reader's Prayer
Heavenly Father,
I come to you in Jesus' name. I receive the wisdom imparted to me through the reading of this book. I pray it helps me draw closer to you, Father. I desire to have the most intimate relationship with you. I know, Father, that the more I know about you, the better my relationship is with you. I love you, Lord. Amen!

Introduction

How did we get to this place of skepticism, and even total waywardness to the God who is, who was and who is to come *"I am Alpha and Omega, the beginning and the ending, saith the Lord, which is, and which was, and which is to come, the Almighty" (Rev. 1:8 KJV)*? This is a question that many have asked in these last days. The answer is simple. Many do not know Him as they ought to because of a lack of teaching and even understanding. *"My people are destroyed for lack of knowledge: because thou hast rejected knowledge, I will also reject thee, that thou shalt be no priest to me: seeing thou hast forgotten the law of thy God, I will also forget thy children" (Hos. 4:6 KJV)*. Notwithstanding, we will take a journey through the Book of books, visiting sites from Genesis to Revelation, and we will be amazingly pleased to learn and reinforce our learning about our great and mighty God. We will explore some characteristics of God, and we will see some things that He cannot do, and that is for our protection because He loves us. You will not have to run after any false because you will know and will recognize the real by knowing God's character. You will know, and you will follow His voice even as Jesus said, *"My sheep hear my voice, and I know them, and they follow me: And I give unto them eternal life; and they shall never perish, neither shall any man pluck them out of my hand" (John 10:27-28 KJV)*.

Afterwards, we will examine different types of mantles, coverings, and the overflow of the Father's heart. You will be able to identify false mantles and false coverings because you will know the authentic. You will see that your Heavenly Father is very approachable, and He designed nothing but the very best for you because He has an expected end for your life. *"For I know the thoughts that I think towards you, saith the Lord, thoughts of peace, and not of evil, to give you and expected end" (Jer. 29:11 KJV).* Then, you will see that you have been fully equipped and deployed to go into all the world and do what you were created to do in the name of the Father, the Son, and the Holy Spirit; knowing that Jesus will never leave you, nor will He ever forsake you: *"Let your conversation be without covetousness; and be content with such things as ye have: for he hath said, I will never leave thee, nor forsake thee" (Heb. 13:5 KJV),* and He will be with you, performing His wonders wherever you go in His Name. Finally, we will conclude with some prayers that will help you to line up with the perfect will of God for your life.

THE PLACE OF SURRENDER

Imagine a place surrounded by trees where a flying mosquito sounds like a landing plane, and where peace is supreme. However, this day, silence has complete reign; as if demanding attention with a soft and gentle voice, yet, authoritatively broke the usual pattern as if eternity stopped to listen, giving its undivided attention to the Most High God. A day sitting on my family room sofa, living a moment that seemed unimportant, where one could even say, be distracted by nothing, and thinking about nothing, so it seemed. The television was on, perhaps for sound and light movement, yet, as if it wasn't there. The Father broke the silence and clearly spoke, and He said, "I am looking for someone who believes like Jesus believed when He walked the face of the earth." With the television on, nonetheless, complete silence governed.

That revelatory moment already in times past from the foundation of the earth became etched in my soul. And in moments like these, one becomes one with eternity's plans and just submits. This twinkling of an eye moment designed to align the course of my walk with the Lord brought visions of the burning bush, the parting of the Red Sea, and the arrest of the moon and the sun. His presence was so sweet and intimate. Knowing that the Maker of the universe, the Father of fathers, and the Lord of lords speaks to His people in such an intimate way, puts things in perspective. In a world of chaos where confusion wants to rule, commanding disruptions and lies, God the Creator silenced all to say, "I am here, I never left you, and I will never leave you. Can you hear me? I chose and called you. I have ordained you. Yes, it is I, your Maker, speaking with you. Pause! Put everything away and listen to me. I love and adore you, and I want to use you in these last hours. I need the faith of Jesus operating in you." Are you listening to the Father right now? Oh, yes, He is telling you the same thing. Will you carry the faith of Jesus in your life, right now? Will you carry the authority, the mantle, the anointing of Jesus, right now? Faith is now! The Father says, "I am the God of now. I am Immanuel-God with you. For so long you have spoken about the God of the past or the God of the future, but I Am the God of now as well. Remember my servant, Moses, who asked me whom shall he say sent him? I am the same yesterday, today, and forever. The past was great, and the future amazing, but now is the time to walk and talk with me. I want to show you things that you do not know." *"Call unto me, and I will answer thee, and show thee great and mighty things, which thou knowest not" (Jer. 33:2 KJV).* "Talk with me, listen to me, and do not be in a hurry to speak. Listen, be a listener. I will teach you my heart's desire. I do not make mistakes. I am speaking to you, the reader, of these sayings. I have you in the palm of my hand. I keep you as the apple of my eyes. My love for you is as a fire shut-up in my bones. I died for you. No greater love exists. I am your light in the darkness, your companion in solitude, and I am He who desires your undivided love, for that is what the mantle demands. I, the Lord, have spoken. Hearken unto my voice and live. I've come to arrest your heart in mine, so you and I are one, and in one accord, with one mind and one purpose and anointing. That is one authority and mantle with one anointing, which is that of my beloved Son, Jesus Christ. Can you hear me? I am knocking at the door of your heart. Open up wide and invite me in, for your eternal journey begins now, and the power and might of my Holy Spirit's resurrection power is yours for the believing, receiving, and operation to bring my sole purpose of changing lives. For this reason, I sent my one and only begotten Son, Jesus, the Christ. Walk with me, talk with me, and work with me. It is not for financial gain; it is all about salvation for the lost." *"For God so loved the world, that he gave his only begotten Son, that whosoever believeth in him should not perish, but have everlasting life" (John 3:16 KJV).* I said, "This is good, Father. I agree with you." That is what God said when He created the heavens and the earth. "It is good." Therefore, I seal this portion of the saying with, "this is good"—God is always good!

God is great, and He does not want us to be deceived. Many live their entire lives searching for a mantle. They run from church to church and from minister to minister looking for their mantle. Unbeknownst to them, they already possess that which they have been searching for. I desire that after you have read this book that you absolutely know and understand that you already have the mantle that you desperately sought after. The Bible talks about getting wisdom, but with wisdom also to get understanding. It is the understanding coupled with wisdom that will guide you in the righteous path the Lord has set before you. Without it, you walk in ignorance aimlessly, and Father God does not want any of

His children to be ignorant. In the book of Hosea, God said that His people perish for lack of knowledge, and that is because they rejected knowledge. *"My people are destroyed for lack of knowledge: because thou hast rejected knowledge, I will also reject thee, that thou shall be no priest to me; seeing thou hast forgotten the law of thy God, I will also forget thy children" (Hos. 4:6 KJV).*

God knows your name, and He knows everything about you. He even knows how many strands of hair are on your head, with none escaping His knowing. God's heart desire is for you to know Him and to live with Him and for Him to the fullest. To this end, He has provided all you will ever need to satisfy the fulfillment of His calling for your life. Knowing your Father God, His Son Jesus Christ, your Lord and Savior, and His precious Holy Spirit will give you a deeper understanding of what is in the mantle that you so desire. This knowledge will propel you to the fulfillment of His calling and ministry in your life. You will not have to stand ashamed before the Father, the Son, nor will you stand ashamed before the Holy Spirit of the Living God.

In the Christian circles, all you hear is about God, Jesus, and the Holy Spirit, but how deep or how profound is your understanding of who this amazing God is? It is up to you to study and to get to know Him in a personal and intimate way. There are no limitations to how close you can get to your Father God, to your Lord and Savior Jesus Christ, and His precious Holy Spirit. Only you can put limitations or dismantle those limitations in your walk with the Lord. No one can tell you how much of God you should know and have. You can only be encouraged or discouraged in your walk with the Lord; however, you have the choice always to choose between good and evil and between the levels of intimacy you must have with your Heavenly Father. In November of 2004, I was in India with an evangelist friend ministering. I was not quite finished ministering at a church during the morning service when a couple of brothers came to pick me up and take me to another church to minister. I did not know about this second engagement. I did not know how far it was from where we were to where we were going. I said to the Lord, "Lord you have from here to there wherever there is to come up with something for your children. Father, I know you do not feed your children old, musty, and hard bread. I need fresh manna from heaven. Lord, I put it in your hands." It wasn't too long before we arrived at the church. They had been worshiping for a while, and they were waiting for me to get there with the Word. I prayed and went right into the message. I had nothing. Of course, I never have anything, but I have learned over the years that the Lord has everything, and His Word is always right and on time. As usual, the Holy Spirit delivered an amazing message and it was "fresh" out of the oven of heaven. I had never heard it before. I wish they had recorded it because I would have loved to hear it and take notes. I say all this to let you know how God operates sometimes, and it is always for our good. That message sparked a hunger in me to know God even more and in greater depth. Since then, I have been on the journey for intimacy with my amazing daddy, my Father God. I knew of Him and I knew Him, but nothing like today, and I pray nothing like tomorrow. The hunger to know my Father God is greater each day.

As a young believer, I had a dream vision. In it, God asked me what I wanted from Him. Sound familiar? This is something like what He asked King Solomon. Oh, I do not claim to be in King Solomon's rank, but I do know that my God does not discriminate, and He is no respecter of a person. This I know because the Bible clearly states it, as you will see in the following Scriptures: *"Then Peter opened his mount, and said, "Of a truth, I perceive that God is no respecter of persons" (Acts 10:34 KJV). "For there is no respect of person with God" (Romans 2:11 KJV),* and, *"But of these who seemed to be somewhat, whatsoever they were, it maketh no matter to me: God accepteth no man's person: for they who seemed to be somewhat in conference added nothing to me" (Gal. 2:6; Eph. 6:9).* Let me continue with the dream vision. In the dream, the Lord asked me what I wanted Him to do for me, and I said to Him, "Lord, I want to know my Father God, Jesus, and your Holy Spirit," and I started to say "and to be happy," but I stopped in the middle of my sentence, because I realized that if I knew the Father, the Son, and the Holy Spirit, I would be happy. Immediately, I woke up. I was in awe! Not too long after that, I had another dream vision. In this one, an angel of the Lord came to me. He had a huge sword in His hand. The fear of God gripped me. I thought, "This is it! I am for sure going to die today. I didn't even have a second to make things right with God." This is one of the reasons one must keep a short account, better yet, empty accounts when it comes to sin with God by living right; and when one falls short, one must be like King David, quick to repent. To my surprise, the sword went in through my umbilical cord, and it came out the same way it went in. I was not hurt, and I was neither in pain nor did any blood come out. It came out as clean and shiny as it had gone in me. I had just gotten a spiritual surgery by the Angel of the Lord. I understood that the Father had deposited His Word in my deepest being, for the Word is called the "sword of the Spirit." *"And take the helmet of salvation, and the sword of the Spirit, which is the word of God" (Eph. 6:17 KJV).* *"For the word of God is quick, and powerful, and sharper than any two-edged sword, piercing even to the dividing asunder of soul and spirit, and of the joints and marrow, and is a discerner of the thoughts and intents of the heart" (Heb. 4:12 KJV).*

Since then, I have had a supernatural hunger for the Word of God. The Lord almost always speaks to me in three. Later, while studying the Word of God, He opened a page in the middle of the

Bible to me, and that same page was opened as I perceived it to be opened seven times. This was an open vision. I was not sleeping, nor was I daydreaming. I was in my "perfect" consciousness. I said, "Wow!" I then said, "Let me put this to test, Holy Spirit." To my amazement, not only did He show me the seven aspects of the page, but He continued to show me that that was just the first level. Remember what Jesus told His disciples about forgiveness, and that is where He took me immediately when He was speaking to me. You see, we cannot put any limitations on God. We only limit ourselves. The journey with God is one of discovery, and daily, we learn new things about our Father God, if only we believe. As a baby Christian, I read about the twenty-four elders, and how they fall and cry "holy, holy, holy" all day long for eternity. I questioned, "how and why?" I wondered what they saw. I now know that every time they look at God the Father, they see something amazing, something new. Our God is the amazing Creator, and I believe He is constantly doing something great and new. He is the Creator, and He cannot do anything other than be Himself and create, create, and create. *"The four and twenty elders fall down before him that sat on the throne, and worship him that liveth forever and ever, and cast their crowns before the throne, saying, Thou art worthy, O Lord, to receive glory and honor and power: for thou hast created all things, and for thy pleasure they are and were created"* (Rev. 4:10-11 KJV). However, there are a few things that the Father cannot do, and I will talk about them as we continue. These things cannot take away from who God is; rather, they explain God differently and especially. Remember, God has no equal, and He can do above all you can ask or imagine from Him in Jesus' name. *"Now unto him, that is able to do exceeding abundantly above all that we ask or think, according to the power that worketh in us"* (Eph. 3:20 KJV).

Let's explore some of God's attributes, character, behavior, and personality. My prayers are that you read this from a godly perspective, and perhaps, apply some of the facts to your life, if you are not already doing so. It is my sincere desire to help my brethren draw closer to our Father, even as I draw closer to Him. Our heavenly Father is God, and beside Him, there are no gods. He is omnipotent, He is omniscient, He is eternal, and He is benevolent. Of course, He is holy, just, and compassionate. In fact, He is matchless. He is all together, and He is eternal as it is so eloquently put: *"Before the mountains were brought forth, or ever thou hadst formed the earth, and the world, even from everlasting to everlasting thou art God" (Ps. 90:2 KJ V)*. He has an indefinite beginning and an indefinite ending.

God is all that and more. Yet, God cannot do all things, or can He? Unlike certain beliefs, God cannot do all things!

What are they, and why is it that God cannot do them? We must understand that God will not violate His Word. There is nothing we can do to change who God is. We cannot change Him no matter how hard we try to make Him something or someone He is not. God operates within the laws and rules He Himself established in His infinite wisdom, and He has chosen to be a God of love, mercy, and of compassion. Thus, He set some things in place that He will not violate for our sake, and I will begin by discussing the God of truth, who cannot lie.

PART I

Getting to Know
God More Intimately

Chapter 1

God Cannot Lie

W e must understand that the God we serve is not a liar. It
is impossible for Him to lie. Consider His creative voice.
If He were to say something contrary to the first, which He does
not, those things would come into an agreement; and thus, manifest and become true. In other words, if God were to look at
the color red and call it blue, that red color would become blue
immediately. Why? It is because He spoke it into existence. In
Genesis 3:15, after Satan's trickery and Adam and Eve's disobedience to God, which we call the fall of mankind, God makes the
promise to redeem us from the kingdom of darkness; and in the
New Testament, He delivers His promise, Jesus Christ, the sacrificial Lamb of God. *"The next day John seeth Jesus coming unto him,
and saith, Behold the Lamb of God, which taketh away the sin of the
world (John 1:29 KJV).*

God is compassionate and faithful. He delivers whatever He
promises because whenever He sends His Word, it will accomplish
whatever He sends it out to perform. These two examples alone
should show you that what He says happens because He cannot lie.
Satan is the liar and the father of lies. God is the Father of truth,
and in Him, there is no evil. *"In hope of eternal life, which God, that
cannot lie, promised before the world began" (Titus 1:2 KJV).* As we
have seen in Titus 1:2, God cannot lie. Also, God is the Creator,

1

and His creative voice causes whatever He says to come to pass. If He says it, you can bank on it. It will come to pass, no ifs and buts about it. Consider the following Scripture, *"God is not a man, that he should lie; neither the son of man, that he should repent: hath he said, and shall he not do it? Or hath he spoken, and shall he not make it good? (Numbers 23:19 KJV).* Furthermore, chapter 6:18 of Hebrews states again that God cannot lie, and because of His truthfulness, we can put our trust and hope in Him. Whatever the Bible says about our present and future in God is absolute truth, and we can rest in full confidence in the God of our salvation. *"That by two immutable things, in which it was impossible for God to lie, we might have a strong consolation, who have fled for refuge to lay hold upon the hope set before us" (Heb. 6:18 KJV).*

In the New Testament, we see that Jesus promised to send the Comforter-the Holy Spirit. This was the same promise that God had made in the Old Testament concerning the outpouring of His Spirit. *"And it shall come to pass afterward, that I will pour out my spirit upon all flesh; and your sons and your daughters shall prophesy, your old men shall dream dreams, your young men shall see visions" (Joel 2:28 KJV).* Jesus commanded the disciples to tarry in Jerusalem until power was given to them from on high. *"And, behold, I send the promise of my Father upon you: but tarry ye in the city of Jerusalem, until ye be endued with power from on high (Lk. 24:49 KVJ).* In the book of Acts chapter two, we see what has been called the Upper Room experience- the day of Pentecost, where the promise of God and Jesus was fulfilled as His disciples were all in one place and one accord. The Holy Spirit of God is the power behind God's mantle for evangelism. He is called the Spirit of Truth. *"Howbeit when he, the Spirit of truth, is come, he will guide you into all truth: for he shall not speak of himself; but whatsoever he shall hear, that shall he speak: and he will shew you things to come" (John 16:13 KJV).* Furthermore, the eight commandments of God prohibit His people from lying, *"Thou shall not bear false witness against thy neighbors" (Ex. 20:16 KJV),* and lying can only come from an unrighteous and unholy mind. God is righteous, and He tells us to be righteous as He is. *"Because it is written, Be ye holy; for I am holy" (I Pet. 1:16 KJV);* those who are God's, practice what God does and is. *"A righteous man hateth lying: but a wicked man is loathsome, and cometh to shame" (Prov. 13:5 KJV).* If a righteous man hates lies, how much more God who is true and truth?

Aren't you glad that our God cannot lie? Therefore, He is not lying to you about what He has done, is doing, and soon will do concerning His plan and His Word. Praise God. Knowing that He cannot lie, brings the peace that surpasses all understanding. *"And the peace of God, which passeth all understanding, shall keep your hearts and minds through Christ Jesus" (Phil. 4:7, KJV).* You can rest assured that His salvation is sure, and you are secured in Him, and in His loving arms, you are kept safe. Believe it. He cannot lie and He cannot change.

Reflection
God Cannot Lie

1. Why is it important for all to know that God cannot lie, especially believers?
2. In a paragraph, talk about your greatest takeaway from this chapter. Tell how you will apply them to your life.

Chapter 2

God Cannot Change

Who will not serve a God who does not change? How many have made vows at their wedding ceremony only to end up breaking their vows and in divorce? The vows, the promises were made, but were they kept? No, soon after the honeymoon is over, the struggles of marriage begin to surface, and before too long, the marriage vows and promises are forgotten, or the spouses "changed" their minds. The husband decides that he never really loved her, or he does not love her anymore. He has found another, who meets all his manly or fleshly desires. Then, on the other side, is the wife, who woke up one morning and "realized" or "discovered" that she doesn't love him either. She never really, really, loved him, and so the best thing for both is to go their separate ways, but not before they torment each other to the maximum. What happened? One might say they changed their minds. Feeble excuses are given. "Well, he is not the man I thought I married." "Oh, yes, she is not my type, and besides, she cannot even cook, nor keep a home." What happened during courtship? Wasn't that the time of discovery and prayers? Oh, I forgot, they were so, "in love." Yes, they were in love.

A brother in Christ asked me to pray for him. He wanted God to show him his wife. No sooner, I began to pray for him, I saw that he had around his stomach area a string with twelve knots, with a person pulling it. I could not see who the person was, but I perceived it was a woman. Each knot represented the women, their family, and the financial commitment he had agreed previously. The string was not tight, and he had wiggle room to move. He seemed to be comfortable in it. It was not suffocating him; hence, he was tempted to live in the mess. I had to cut all the ungodly connections in prayer for him to be set free and become in alignment with God so he could find his wife. The Bible says that he, the man who finds a wife, finds a good thing and is blessed by the Lord. *"Whoso findeth a wife findeth a good thing and obtaineth favour of the LORD" (Prov. 18:22 KJV).* Therefore, if the wife is not from God, she cannot be a blessing. I asked him to fast and pray so the Lord could show him his helpmeet. Sometimes, it is easy for men and women to break their promises, even promises made before God. What they do not understand is that it is not just a physical or natural connection, it is also a spiritual alignment that can only be broken through prayer. Leaving one relationship and stepping into another without breaking the previous covenant leaves you vulnerable and entangled, and until you break the soul ties, you are still connected and cannot move forward in God. Repent and ask God for forgiveness and live in peace within. You must take responsibility for the wrong alliance and for breaking your vows, which tie you to the person or persons. I am going to pause here to address the connection of soul ties, and to help you get set free should you need to, so you can have a happy life with your spouse. You see, when you break up your relationship with the person but do not break the soul ties or emotional baggage with that person or persons, you bring that person and every other person he or she has been in relationships before you into your new relationship. You start a new relationship with all the intentions and hope that this time it will work. You try your best to make it work, but it seems that you are repeating history.

Then, you wonder why it is not working. It does not work because you are not just having a relationship with this new person, but also with all the people both you and this new person has been involved in the past. Consider the following:

You have been married and divorced once, or you had a boyfriend or girlfriend whom you dated for years, but never married the person. You ended that relationship and moved on to the next. Regardless if it was a wife/husband or boy/girlfriend, there were a set of persons, him or her, his or her family, and the financial responsibilities. You did not break the soul ties with this person and moved on, carrying the person, the family, and financial responsibilities. You also carried all the boyfriends or girlfriends this person had ever had, not to mention the set of demons they hosted. How many are your carrying at this point? How heavy is your baggage? Who knows? It can be a set of three or sets of hundreds, and each time you move from one relationship to another without breaking soul ties, you add to the chain, making it more extensive, stronger, and harder to control and to break. Now, suppose you are a gentleman, and you have found your wife as the Bible states. You want to become one with her, but how can you when you have brought so many, and she has brought her own set to the marriage? You want an agreement with your wife, but many voices are speaking. You are confused. You do not know if you are listening to the present voice or voices in your past. You know that the Bible says that the two of you are to become one, and you desperately want to be in one accord. How can you accomplish this? You asked. I am glad. Here is what you have to do. Ask the Holy Spirit to bring to your remembrance all your past relationships and take care of breaking the soul ties chain. I recommend beginning with the most recent relationship, and all the persons this person ever had a relationship with before you. It doesn't matter if they were men or women. Break the connection and destroy the ungodly alliances in Jesus' name, by repenting and asking God to forgive you, forgive the person and his or her chain, and forgive yourself; and then ask the Holy Spirit to collect all the scattered pieces of your life shared with them, to cleanse them, make them holy before the Father, Son, and Holy Spirit, and then, to bring them back to you, making you whole in that area. You follow these steps for each relationship you have ever had until you have completely finished every ungodly connection. You are to do this with emotional ties as well as spiritual. Demonic forces tend to trespass and attach themselves to us in areas that we do not even realize, but the Holy Spirit is the revealer of all things. They cannot possess a Christian, but they sure can attach themselves in some parts of our bodies without permission. Some incurable diseases are due to the soul ties condition. Sometimes we give attention to those we should not, and that can become soul ties as well; so if you have someone like that in your past, take care of it as well. You want to come clean to your spouse so you can become one with each other, and with the Father, Son, and Holy Spirit. That is the only way you will have the godly relationship God ordained for you and your spouse. Many marriages will survive and thrive when both persons take time to prayerfully break every tie with their past relationships. You are probably thinking that if you break soul ties with just the person you were involved with that it suffices, but what about the cobwebs that sprung from the previous relationships? Haven't you heard someone say that this person does not do things like the previous one? They say this without thinking how much that statement hurt their current mate. This leads to resentment, the death of romantic relationships. Why are they expecting you to behave like the previous lover? Soul ties were not broken. Did you not say to someone, "I found my soulmate?" Yes, you have heard those words. The wrong soulmate; therefore, you must break ties with the person or persons if you want to live that happy married life you deserve and God-ordained for both of you. Believe me when I tell you that it works. Whether or not you decide to take a spouse now or later, you are free from all past hurts, and you can become that good wife or husband God's son or daughter needs to fulfill God's calling in your life. Many keep looking back to their past relationships even though they were awful. They can't seem to leave their past behind. That is soul ties. Break them and walk in freedom and liberty. No marriage is perfect, but you will be able to communicate with one another with love and respect and will solve all the issues that may come up in a godly fashion because you are one body and will love and respect each other as God designed. Don't break your vows to each other, break soul ties.

Allow God to be your example and be faithful to one another. God does not change: *"Jesus Christ the same yesterday, and today and forever"* (Hebrews 13:8 KJV), and *"But thou art the same, and they years shall never end"* (Ps. 102:27 KJV). *"Every good gift and every perfect gift is from above, and cometh down from the Father of lights, with whom is no variableness, neither shadow of turning"* (James 1:17 KJV). God is God, and beside Him, there is none. Moses had an awesome relationship with God, and in his prayer, he leaves us an amazing statement of God's existence. *"Before the mountains were brought forth, or ever thou hadst formed the earth and the world, even from everlasting to everlasting, thou art God"* (Ps. 90:2 KJV).

Balaam and Balak is a great story to examine when settling in your heart that God is unchangeable. Balak, the king of Moab, wanted to curse the Israelites whom God had blessed. At first, we see Balaam, a non-Israelite prophet, who used divination, refusing to go to Balak for the sole purpose of cursing God's chosen people. However, like the devil, Balak is so persistent that Balaam gives in almost to his demise, as we all know well of the ass who saw the Angel of the Lord with His sword drawn, ready to strike Balaam dead, and the ass refused to move, and was struck by Balaam, causing it to speak to the mad prophet and saving his life. Balaam, in the end, tells Balak that he cannot do what he was asking him to do, according to Numbers chapters 23-24. You see, God had blessed, and Balaam could not, nor anyone else, curse those God had blessed, and the Lord was not going to reverse His Word. He knows what He does, and He does not reverse or change His mind. He is sovereign.

There is another account where the people were blessed because they followed the first and the only correct Word of God in their lives. The Rechabites were told by the prophet Jeremiah, who was a true prophet of God, to drink wine. Nonetheless, they already had the Word of the Lord working for them, and they knew that they were not permitted to drink wine forever. Although Jeremiah was a true prophet, they understood the word, *forever*. *"And Jeremiah said unto the house of the Rechabites, Thus saith the Lord of hosts, the God of Israel; Because ye have obeyed the commandment of Jonadab your father, and kept all his precepts, and done according unto all that he hath commanded you: Therefore thus saith the Lord of hosts, the God of Israel; Jonadab the son of Rechab shall not want a man to stand before me forever" (Jer. 35:18-19 KJV)*. They refused to follow the second word because they knew that God does not change His mind, and it was counted as righteousness for them, and God promised that because of their obedience based on their knowledge of His unchanging character, He promised them to have a place in His presence forever. No drinking wine forever obedience gave them a place in God's presence. You must know and understand this principle to obey the Word of God in your life. If God speaks to you, and someone comes to you with a different word that appeases the flesh, you must know to obey the spiritual Word and refuse the flesh. Jesus said that many false Christs and prophets would come to deceive us. Therefore, we must know God's character.

In Malachi, we see how God made provision in His Word, even before time, so that we are not destroyed in His anger toward our sins. God is good, and there is no doubt. He loves us, and He cares very much for His children. *"For I am the LORD, I change not; therefore, ye sons of Jacob are not consumed" (Mal. 3:6 KJV).* I am so grateful for His mercy. In a world where everything is not what it seems, we can rest assured and be in peace, knowing that the Bible, the Word of God, tells us exactly what is true and unchangeable. The Bible is the one and only thing we can trust to be what it is, and we can trust in what it says because it is backed up by the God who cannot lie, the God who cannot change, and the God who does not break His promises.

Reflection
God Cannot Change

1. In the soul ties prayer, how many knots did the string have, and who and what did they represent?
2. Why was it important for him to agree with the prayer, cutting his ungodly alliances?
3. According to Proverbs 18:22, what does he who finds a wife find?
4. What significance does the breaking of ungodly ties have?
5. What does Hebrews 13:8 say about Jesus?
6. What does Moses say about God in Psalm 90:2? Why is this knowledge important to comprehend? Explain.
7. Can those who God has blessed be cursed? Why? Why not?
8. Explain why the Rechabites did not listen to Jeremiah's prophetic word to them.

9. According to Malachi 3:6, why does God not change?
10. What is your take on the statement, "God cannot change?"

Chapter 3

God Cannot Break a Promise

People lie and make promises that they cannot keep, nor do they intend to keep. Years ago, as a young child growing up on the Island of São Nicolau, Cabo-Verde on the West Coast of Africa where I was born, traveling from my village to another nearby village, I met an elderly man. He wore a beautiful straw hat. I loved his hat, so, I complimented him on it. As a child, and still to this day, I am not a shy person. I am an extrovert who will strike a conversation with anyone willing to converse with me. So, I did that day with the man, and I will call him Nho Antone. He then proceeded to tell me that his hat was pregnant and that when it gave birth, he would give me a baby hat. Furthermore, he told me to come back for my baby hat the following week. I took him at his word. Week after week, I went to his house to see if his hat had hatched the little hats. Now, you may be thinking that I was not too bright and that I should have known that hats do not reproduce, but what you don't know is that I knew that hats did not reproduce, but I thought that the man would make me a hat, and I went along with his game, pretending that his hat would reproduce little hats. Thus, I would get my little hat. It was a game to him, but at first, to me as well. It was a matter of a promise that did not get fulfilled. Weeks turned to months, and I settled in my heart that it was never going to happen. You see, every week has a "next week," and the next week never arrives, for when it arrives, it will be this week and not next week; the games people play with children. The man may have thought that his game was funny and that it was a form of entertainment for him, especially on an island where nothing much happened then. Nho Antone was to be a promise-breaker and a liar; a person without integrity, who could not be trusted. It sounds strong, I know.

How many times has someone made a promise to you, game or not, and did not follow through? Life is full of disappointments, right? Yes, but we children of God must be careful of the things we promise people, especially children. I remember my mom would always say, "Do not promise anything to anyone if you do not intend to make it true, especially children, because they do not forget, and they will hold you to it." *"Better is it that thou shouldest not vow, than that thou shouldest vow and not pay" (Eccl. 5:5 KJV).* I think of those words often, and I do my very best not to break promises. The Bible tells us that it is better not to make a promise than to make it and then break it. It's best to submit to the leading of the Holy Spirit and follow in our Heavenly Father's footsteps. He does not break His promises.

I am so glad that God cannot break a promise. *"My covenant will I not break, nor alter the thing that is gone out of my lips" (Ps. 89:34 KJV).* Not only does God not break His promise to us, but He also will not alter it either. God does not promise us one thing and delivers another. What He promises to do, He will do. Now, that doesn't mean that we do not misinterpret His Word at times, but that is our error, not His delivery. Sometimes we want God to do something for us, and we want it so fast and so bad, that we step in to help Him make it come to pass. When it turns out to be something different, we want to blame God. Look at Abraham and Sarah. God promised them a child. Instead of them waiting on God, they went ahead of God, believing they were helping God;

and look at what happened: two sons, one son of the free woman, or wife, and the other from the bondwoman or the slave woman. Did God not deliver the promised son? Oh, yes, He did. Isaac was the promise God made to Sarah and Abraham, not Ismael. And we see what happened down the road. God does not need our help to fulfill His promises. He just needs us to trust Him and to take Him at His Word. He will not break His promises. I am so glad because I know His salvation for my life is sure, and it is secured in Him. You must know that your salvation is sure in Him (Gen. 12-25)! One of my favored Scriptures, and one given to me as a baby Christian in a dream, is one that I hold on to in good times and in bad times. *"I am Alpha and Omega, the beginning and the ending, saith the Lord, which is, and which was, and which is to come, the Almighty" (Rev. 1:8 KJV).* This Scripture is a faith builder. I can read it, quote it, meditate on it, pray it, and it just gives me that surpassing all-understanding peace as I walk with my Lord. I know beyond a shadow of a doubt, He will not change on me. He is constant, and I can rely on, trust, and believe Him to do whatever He has spoken in my life. Because of His unchanging character, I have been in places that otherwise, I would not dream of going. I have this sense of pure and innocent trust and confidence in Him. At times, it is scary, but in a good way. I have even said to Him, "Father, I am doing this just because I trust you." How awesome is it to feel and to know that God never leaves you, nor does He forsake you? I have this engraved in my heart, and I believe it with all my heart. I remember walking up a high place where many tourists walk up to the top to have a bird's view of the city, and on the highest point, there was a banner where people wrote their names on to say that they were there. I did a similar thing, but what I wrote was, "Jesus is the Lord of lords." This was a bold action, but I did it because I was inspired by the Holy Spirit. Soon after I wrote it, I was attacked on my right thigh, and I limped in pain for a couple of days. I knew what had happened, and I was not concerned, because I recognized the attack. I just prayed for the pain to go in Jesus' name, and within a couple of days, I was completely free. Many innocently participate in activities like that, not knowing that they are opening a door to the enemy in their lives. I declared that Jesus is Lord of lords instead of the demons worshiped in that place. The Lord kept me that day, and He will keep me always. You see, the blood of Jesus is a mighty weapon against the enemy because it protects us immediately upon our calling on the Blood. I used the Blood that day as I always do. I am here to tell you that we are more than conquerors through Christ Jesus. The Blood works, and our God does not lie, nor does He change like shifting shadows. He is immovable! *"Every good gift and every perfect gift is from above, and cometh down from the Father of lights, with whom is no variableness, neither shadow of turning"* (*Ja. 1:17 KJV*). God will not break His covenant. *"And yet for all that, when they be in the land of their enemies, I will not cast them away, neither will I abhor them, to destroy them utterly, and to break my covenant with them: for I am the LORD their God"* (*Lev. 26:44 KJV*). I like Jeremiah's prayer. He reminds God of His promises. *"Do not abhor us, for thy name's sake; do not disgrace the throne of thy glory. Remember, break not thy covenant with us"* (*Jer. 14:21 KJV*). Isn't it awesome to know that we can bring to God His own Word, and He keeps that which He has said and promised? I love to remind the Father of His Word in prayer. Number one, it is good to speak His Word, especially to Him. He is faithful to fulfill His promises. He delights in fulfilling His promises to His children. Are you not a child of God? If you are not, stop here and just ask Jesus to come into your life and become your Lord and Savior; believe me, He will. It is that simple. Jesus said if the earthly fathers who are evil give good gifts to their children, how much more will God the Father, who is Holy? *"If ye then being evil, know how to give good gifts unto your children: how much more shall your heavenly Father give of the Holy Spirit to them who ask him" (Luke 11:13 KJV).* Let us not allow the sin of doubt to enter our minds and hearts, and sin against our good God and Father. When you find yourself doubting in an area of your life, just ask Him to help you. Don't allow guilt and condemnation to settle in. God is faithful to forgive you when you ask Him, and He is willing to help you overcome those areas of unbelief. Just be honest with yourself and with Him. After all, He is all-knowing. *"Thus saith the Lord: if ye can break my covenant of the day, and my covenant of the night, and that there should not be day and night in their season Then may also my covenant be broken and with David my servant, that he should not have a son to reign upon his throne; and with the Levites, the priests, my ministers" As the host of heaven cannot be numbered, neither the sand of the sea measured: so will I multiply the seed of David my servant, and the Levites that minister unto me" (Jer. 33:20-22 KJV).* God gave a challenge to men in these Scriptures. If you can break the covenant of the day and the night, then He can break His covenant with King David and his offspring. We all know that no one can break the day and night covenant of God. If it could be done, some scientists, who believe to be gods, would have done so long ago. You and I both know that men can't break this covenant. So, my thoughts are God is God, and beside Him, there is none. Some may claim to be god, some may even want to be god, but in the end, they are just players without games in the walk of life. Why not be respectful and grateful to the God who can and has kept His promises in the past, knowing that He will keep all His promises concerning His children, and His plan of salvation for all in the future? I love the fact that my God is the promise keeper, who is truthful and trustworthy.

Reflection
God Cannot Break a Promise

1. What Does the Bible teach concerning promises?
2. Does God break or alter His promises?
3. Does God need our help in fulfilling His promises to us. Why or why not?
4. What is one mighty weapon of protection God has given us against the enemy?
5. Sight a few Scriptures that confirm that God does not change.
6. Name the covenant that cannot be broken according to Jeremiah 33:20-22.
7. Who is our promise keeper, and how does this knowledge make you feel?
8. Summarize this chapter and tell how it is applicable to your life.

Chapter 4

God's Word Cannot Be Destroyed

T he Word of God cannot be broken, nor can it be destroyed. It cannot end, and it cannot pass away, as stated in Matthew, *"Heaven and earth shall pass away, but my words shall not pass away" (Matt. 24:35 KJV)*. The Word does what it is sent out to do. Isaiah explains it plainly, *"...So shall my word be that goeth forth out of my mouth: it shall not return unto me void, but it shall accomplish that which I please, and it shall prosper in the thing whereto I sent it" (Isa. 55:8 KJV)*. John tells us why the Word cannot be destroyed, nor can it pass away. He says that the Word of God and God are one. *"In the beginning was the Word and the Word was with God and the Word was God" (John 1:1 KJV)*. Furthermore, the Bible tells us that the Word and Jesus are one. Obviously, since God the Father, God the Son, and God the Holy Spirit are one with the Word, the Word cannot be destroyed.

Otherwise, God, Himself, could be destroyed. And that is impossible. The Word of God is powerful all by itself. *"And the Word was made flesh and dwelt among us, and we beheld his glory, the glory as the only begotten of the Father full of grace and truth" (John 1:14 KJV); and Jesus said, "I and my Father are one" (John 10:30 KJV)*.

Although many have come against the Word of God, and many have misused it to their evil intent and interests, regardless, it cannot be destroyed. If that could happen, men would have done it many moons ago. Being that the Word is a mirror, it shows us things that at times we do not want to know, and we do not want to deal with, whether it is for our good or demise. One thing that I say to my brothers and sisters is that it is time for us to use the Word of God for our benefit and that of others to bring them to the salvation knowledge of Jesus Christ, our Lord and Savior. Witches and warlocks and other evil ones use the Word even against us Christians. The Masonic, amongst other false religions, use the Word of God because they know it works. Years ago, a young man involved in the Masonic activities bragged about their use of Scriptures in their rituals and how ignorant "Christians" are of the power in the Word of God, as if I did not know that they use it in their rituals. He was shocked at the depth of my knowledge and understanding concerning their activities. His pride and arrogance were his trap. However, it is time for some Christians to wake up and take what is rightfully theirs. Believers must teach and preach the unaltered Gospel. Let's do it, and watch signs and wonders follow as the Word declares. *"And they went forth, and preached everywhere, the Lord working with them, and confirming the word with signs following. Amen" (Mark 16:20 KJV).*

We know the Word cannot be destroyed; we know the Word is powerful; we know the Word works, so let's be confident, and with faith, boldly come to the Throne of Grace and bombard heaven with our confident prayers. I remember one day, as I was talking to the Father, and He said, "All prayers begin with me." Of course, He was talking about His will. I said to Him, "Prove it to me." This is how I talk to the Father. He knows I mean no disrespect. It was He who taught me not to hide from my flesh as it is written, *"Is it not to deal thy bread to the hungry, and that thou bring the poor that are cast out to thy house? When thou seest the naked, that thou cover him; and that thou hide not thyself from thine own flesh" (Isa. 58:7 KJV)*? He said the most surprising Scripture to me. He said, "John 3:16." I said, "John 3:16?" And I went ahead and quoted it to Him, *"For God so loved the world that he gave his only begotten Son, that whosoever believeth in him should not perish, but have everlasting life" (John 3:16 KJV).* I stopped in the middle of the Scripture with "He gave." I said, "Wow, Lord! You are so right." Of course, He is always right. When have you ever seen God wrong? Never! I said, "Okay, there is always the witness of two or three. Where is the other Scripture?" He said, "Isa. 54:3." *"For thou shalt break forth on the right hand and on the left, and thy seed shall inherit the Gentiles and make the desolate cities to be inhabited." And he also gave me this Scripture. "Arise, shine; for thy light is come, and the glory of the LORD is risen upon thee" (Isa. 60:1 KJV).* One could say that these Scriptures do not line up with the topic of prayer beginning in the Father's heart, but oh, yes, they do. Jesus is the begotten Son, Jesus is the Seed that was given, and Jesus is the Light. I had no questions and no doubt. If anyone could destroy the Word, Satan would have done it already. He couldn't, and he cannot. He has attempted to manipulate it as he did with Adam and Eve with his, "Did God say?" and tried with Jesus and his, "If you are the Son of God..." Believe me when I tell you, believe the Bible, believe God. His Word cannot be demolished. It cannot be destroyed, nor can it be smashed. It cannot be wrecked, nor devastated, and it certainly cannot be ruined. It will stand forever as the Bible says, *"Thy kingdom come, Thy will be done in earth, as it is in heaven" (Matt. 6:10 KJV).* So, put it to work in faith, and watch God honor His Word in your life and the lives of those around you. Pray from heaven's perspective and not from your viewpoint. God is always supreme! Let it be done in the earth as it is in heaven.

Reflection
God's Word Cannot Be Destroyed

1. Why is it that the Word of God cannot be destroyed?

Chapter 5

God's Word Cannot Be Null and Void

It behooves us to pay attention to the Word of God. The Bible talks about power in the tongue. How many times have you said something negative and it came to pass? I know I have. We were created in God's image, and He gave us the Scriptures, and they tell us to speak to one another of that which is good and lovely. *"Speaking to yourselves in psalms and hymns and spiritual songs, singing and making melody in your heart to the Lord" (Eph. 5:19 KJV).* We must bless one another. Most of the time when people try to speak some ungodly mess into my life, I rebuke those words, and I do not receive them in Jesus' name. I render them powerless and burn them to crisp; then, I scatter them, so they can never come together to harm me or my loved ones. I know that the Word of God, once it is sent out, it will accomplish what it is sent out to do. Evildoers sometimes use the Word of God to perform their evil deeds. They know the power of the spoken Word of God. The Bible is a weapon, and we must use it when fighting the enemy. It is the sword of the Spirit. *"And take the helmet of salvation, and the sword of the Spirit, which is the word of God" (Eph. 6:17 KJV).* The Word of God is also quick and powerful. It is also sharper than any double-edged sword. It does what it says. If you have any doubt, try reading the Bible when you are living in sin. It will convict you, and you will feel so uncomfortable until you repent and make things right with God. I know for a fact that it is true. I cannot read the Bible if I feel wrong about something or anyone. I must repent, ask for forgiveness, and when possible, go and make things right with the person before I can really study the Bible. The conviction is very strong. I am glad that God chooses to use His Word to convict me. *"For the word of God is quick, and powerful and sharper than any two-edged sword, piercing even to the dividing asunder of soul and spirit, and of the joints and marrow, and is a discerner of the thoughts and intents of the heart" (Heb. 4:12 KJV).* He loves us so much. Thank God for choosing to correct us through His Word. I am so happy to serve a God whose word cannot be null, nor can it be void. I can live in perfect harmony by putting my trust in Him and His Word.

God's Word is true. You can bank on it, I have. One way is through obedience to His firstfruits, tithe, and offering principles. There were times I did not know where the mortgage payment was coming from, and God would take me to this Scripture: *"Take therefore no thought for the morrow: for the morrow shall take thought for the things of itself. Sufficient unto the day is the evil thereof" (Matt. 6:34 KJV).* And this Scripture would put my concerns to rest. I would feel at peace and assured that all was well, and it would turn out to be what He promised in His Word. I take God at His Word.

God's Word is exactly what it says. *"Thy word is true from the beginning: and every one of thy righteous judgments endureth forever" (Ps. 119:160 KJV).* There is no need to try to confuse it. It is very plainly written. All you must do is exercise your faith in God and His Word, and you will be as He says; no matter what may happen to you, you are more than conquerors through Christ Jesus. *"As it is written, For thy sake we are killed all the day long; we* are accounted as sheep for the slaughter. *"Nay, in all these things we are more than conquerors through him that loved us" (Rom. 8:36-37 KJV).* King David said in *"The works of his hands are verity and judgment; All his commandments are sure. O God, my heart is fixed; I will sing and give praise, even with my glory" (Ps.111:7-8 KJV).* What then shall you do? You shall praise and worship your God and Father for His mighty Word. Jesus gives us great teaching in the following verses of Scripture. He did not come to destroy the Word. Remember from previous chapters, the Word or the Law of God cannot be destroyed. Rather, He came to fulfill it as it was prophesied in the Old Testament about Him. *"Think not that I am come to destroy the law or the prophets: I am not come to destroy, but to fulfill. For verily I say unto you, Till heaven and earth pass, one jot or one tittle shall in no wise pass from the law, till all be fulfilled" (Matt. 5:17-18 KJV).* Not only couldn't the Word be destroyed, but it also will never end either. Heaven and earth may pass, but not one little thing in the Bible will pass away. Again, the Bible, the Word of God, and God the Father and the Son are one. Therefore, the Word of God can't be destroyed. *"And it is easier for heaven and earth to pass, than one tittle of the law to fail" (Luke 16:17 KJV).*

The apostle Paul says that we are here on earth to establish the law of God, not to abolish it. *"Do we then make void the law through faith? God forbid: yea, we establish the law" (Rom. 3:31 KJV).* God's law is perfect, and it is just. Therefore, we enforce it on earth for the benefit of mankind. Jesus Christ, the Word of God, is forever the same. He does not change. *"Jesus Christ the same yesterday, and today, and forever" (Heb. 13:8 KJV).*

Reflection
God's Word Cannot Be Null and Void

1. Give a reason why it is vitally important to watch what you say.
2. What do you do when people try to speak things contrary to God's Word into your life?
3. Describe the Word of God according to Hebrews 4:12.
4. What do you need to exercise the Word of God powerfully?
5. According to Matthew 5:17-18, why did Jesus come?
6. According to Apostle Paul in Romans 3:31, why are we here on earth?

Chapter 6

God Cannot Stop Loving His People

G od is love; therefore, He cannot stop loving His people. *"He that loveth not knoweth not God; for God is love" (I John 4:8 KJV)*. We see God's greatest act of love in His giving of Jesus Christ, His one and only begotten Son. *"For God so loved the world, that he gave his only begotten Son, that whosoever believeth in him should not perish, but have everlasting life" (John 3:16 KJV)*. In Jesus, God made a way of escape for those who love Him and accept His Son as Lord and Savior. Jesus is the way, the truth, and the life, and without Him, there is no passage to heaven. *"Jesus saith unto him, I am the way, the truth, and the life: no man cometh unto the Father, but by me" (John 14:6 KJV)*. No one will come to the Father who will not go through the portal that God has provided. There are no side doors, nor are there any back windows. Would you have offered your only son to die for the world? Think about it. God did. Why did He do it? He did it because He is love, and He cannot stop loving His people. He is the good God, and He is the good Father. None can compare with His matchless love. This agape love is not something you work for; it isn't something you earn. It is the gift of God. Jesus is His greatest gift of love to us. Please do not attempt to cheapen His gift. In the end, you will lose all and you will be sorry, but at what expense? Let your heart believe. It is in you to believe because God put it in you by giving you a measure of faith. He is just, and He is holy. He will not ask you for something He hasn't provided in the first place. He will not ask you either for something you cannot give to Him. Don't be stubborn. Pride comes before a fall. Please stand! Stand tall and don't let pride and arrogance rob you of eternal life with God. *"Pride goes before destruction and a haughty spirit before a fall" (Prov. 16:18 KJV).* Do not be deceived. Satan, the enemy of your soul, is the one who has been lying to you. He has been telling you that God does not exist. Why? Satan lies to you because Satan wants you in hell with him. Know that you were created by God for heaven. He is your Heavenly Father. God loves you so much. He is calling you to His bosom even now. Do you feel His tugging at your heart? Don't ignore it. It is your Father's heart beating in yours. Respond to Him. Just tell Him, "Yes." It is that simple. God is love, and He is merciful. Put your trust in Him. He will forgive and deliver you from all unrighteousness, and He will draw you close to Him. *"Who is a God like unto thee, that pardoneth iniquity and passeth by the transgression of the remnant of his heritage? He retaineth not his anger forever, because he delighteth in mercy" (Mic. 7:18 KJV).*

How many times has God sent someone your way to help you in a difficult situation, and you refuse because it did not look like what you thought it should look like? Then, you accuse Him of not loving you or being the love He is? Open your heart and let Him in. God is love! *"Beloved, let us love one another: for love is of God; and every one that loveth is born of God, and knoweth God. He that loveth not knoweth not God; for God is love" (I John 4:7-8 KJV).* Let the Father shower you with His unconditional agape love.

There are several types of love, and at times, people confuse them; however, Christians cannot afford the luxury. Consequently,

I will discuss them briefly because more than ever, we need genuine love in our lives and our churches; but how can we affectionately display love if we do not have a clear understanding of what love is? We must know and understand the kind of love we and the world need. Looking at the different types of love carefully will help us to focus on the kind of love we want for ourselves and the kind of love others desperately need. The Church must impart love like Jesus did. He commanded us to love one another; therefore, it is important to know the different types of love, especially the feelings behind each state of love. Another important aspect of love is the use of it. *I love you* should be used only when addressing feelings and not likes. For example, I enjoy coffee. I am passionate about my job, instead of using I *love* coffee, or I *love* my job. Feelings are controlled by the right side of the brain and language by the left. If you use the word *love* too often and out of context, it will lose its potency. Hence, you must use the expression of love when you are referring to feelings and not likes. Love is a strong emotion. Put it into action, and you get what you put in.

Once we have learned how to feel and cultivate our love, we can share our love with others. We must learn and know about the different situations of love. Recognize them when we are feeling them because only then can we share what we possess. The love between two people can only begin if the interaction is based on mutual respect, truth, and trust. This is vitally important in relationships. When both persons are engaged in a relationship forged out of truth, respect, and trust, both feel love, and their love can grow because both are investing in the relationship equally. Remember that it is easy to fall in love, but how will you stay in love? If it is too difficult to stay in love, it must not be the love of your life because love is always beautiful. If it is not beautiful, it must not be love. In other words, love does not do ugly as is seen in God's Word (I Cor. 13:1-13).

God's unconditional agape love is best described as the holiest and purest form of a love of all, and of all times. It expresses a human virtue that is based on compassion, affection, and kindness. This is a state of being that has nothing to do with something or someone outside one's self. It is all about the God within. The God who gave His life and died, and in a brutal way for mankind, and there is no greater love than this love. *"Greater love hath no man than this, that a man lay down his life for his friends" (John 15:13, KJV)."For God so loved the world, that he gave his only begotten Son, that whosoever believeth in him should not perish, but have everlasting life" (John 3:16 KJV).* The Father's love cannot be confused with the eros love, nor can it be compared with any other.

The eros type of love is best described as the love of the body or sexual desires. It is also said to be of "divine" beauty or lust. This love is an animalistic type of love that exercises no self-control, nor does it have a rationale for the engagement. It is almost pure madness. Eros is the Greek god of lust, as is Cupid, the Latin god of lust. They are the same spirit, who control human minds and emotions, and if not careful, the individual can submit to this spirit and is used as ponds. Years ago, there was a movie released titled *Incubus*, and of course, its sibling was Succubus. Both are the evil spirit of lust. This spirit has existed for ages, but many ignore their signs and are in bondage by them. Many years ago, I was asked to minister on deliverance. At first, I was reluctant because I knew what the Holy Spirit wanted me to minister on. The topic was the spirit of lust. Of course, I submitted and went ahead and did what the Lord wanted. At the end of the sermon, I made an altar call. The altar was packed. Many came up for prayer. What happened next, only God knew and could deliver. Many were delivered from the eros spirit. Husbands and wives were delivered, and families were restored. I remember a young couple who was having marital problems, and after she confessed that she had not been intimate with her husband for a long time and that he thought that she was having an affair. Well, she was, but it wasn't the typical extramarital affair. She had been having sexual dreams; and in them, she was being sexually satisfied by demons; therefore, she did not need to be intimate with her husband. The demons had entered into her through sexual molestation at a young age; and later, reinforced their ownership of her through multiple rapes. I am so glad the Lord set her free from those demonic forces that night. Over the years, I have ministered to many who have these types of dreams and think they are being intimate with the face they see in their dreams. But I say, if you pay close attention to them, you will see that there is something not quite right about the person's image. You are not dreaming of intimacy with that person, it is a familiar spirit that has infiltrated your dreams and is being intimate with you and not the person you think. Just ask the Lord to forgive you and to set you free. There is no shame in admitting you have had this problem. The shame is in continuing to engage in something you know is wrong according to God's Word. After this, you know the truth, and now you cannot play the innocent card. I remember a time when a demon came to me in my dream, and it had my husband's face. There was just something about it that was not right. I recognized it to be a familiar spirit. I said to the demon, "If I want intimacy, all I need to do is wake up and ask my husband." With those words, it changed its form, and it showed its true self-a demon, and it disappeared as a dark puff of smoke in the air. You must be wise as serpents and gentle as doves. *"Behold, I send you forth as sheep in the midst of wolves: be therefore wise as serpents, and harmless as doves" (Matt. 10:16 KJV).* Remember, God always gives us a way of escape out of ungodly situations. He gives us true friends that we can call on for help in times of need as well. Stay free from demonic influences. If you have been having these types of dreams, pray before going to bed, and ask Jesus to set you free. Plead the blood of Jesus and know that the Blood works. Just call on the blood in Jesus' name. *Philia* is an ancient Greek word for love. It is often translated as brotherly, friendship, or affectionate love, and its complete opposite is called *phobia*. No one in his or her right mind chooses to live life without friends, even if all other needs are adequately met because friendship is necessary for a happy life. Friendships can be divided into three types: good, utility, and pleasure, or it can be said as a friend for a reason, friendships of utility, a friend for a season, friendships of pleasure, and a friend for a lifetime, friendships of the good. Friendships of the good is true friendship, and it is the highest level of friendship. Both friends enjoy each other's characters and company. A true friend thinks of the friend's needs before his or her own. The motive behind this friendship is the care for the friend, and when both friends keep similar characters, the relationship will thrive and endure. It is a long-lasting relationship. You can look at the relationship between Ruth and Naomi. Ruth could have left Naomi, but she chose to stay and take care of her mother-in-law, even though Naomi gave her permission to leave and go back to her father's house after her husband died. Ruth chose to stay and make Naomi's God her own and look at how God blessed her with a new husband and one on Jesus' line. *"And Ruth said, Entreat me not to leave thee, or to return from following after thee, for whither thou goest, I will lodge: thy people shall be my people. And thy God my God" (Ruth 1:16 KJV).* The friendship of utility, or better put, acquaintances, is friendship based on interest or business. Once the business has been executed, the friendship is over. These people may never see or speak to each other again unless there is a need for further transactions. And the friendships of pleasure are based on mutual interests, and s/he delights in the company of the other person. These friends do part once their interests change and no longer enjoy the same activities or each other's company.

Another type of love is that of Ludus, which is a playful love or flirting. Most of us have heard the expression of playing with fire. And we know that those who play with fire, sooner or later, will get burned. Samson's flirting with Delilah is a good example of this type of love (Judges 16). He began by flirting and teasing, and before he knew it, Delilah had the best of him, and it cost him everything, including his very own life. It is dangerous whether you are on the giving or receiving end. This is also when you find what has been called "fatal attraction," and many lives have been destroyed by interpretation or misinterpretation of the flirtation. The best thing is never to start, but should you find yourself flirting, quit while you're ahead. Delilah was the wrong woman for Samson because she was a Philistine, the enemy of the Israelite. It was not a match made in heaven like Isaac and Rebekah.

Pragma is the love between husband and wife, and it is based on love and respect. According to Ephesian 5:23-33, husbands are to love their wives as Christ loves the Church and gave His life for it, and wives are to respect their husbands. I have always said that if a wife knows that her husband loves her, that she would go to war with him and for him. Women need to be loved, even as the Church needs to be loved by Christ. Telling the wife that she is loved is equally important as showing her that she is loved. Husbands, never assume that your wife knows that you love her, just tell her while you are showing her. Even if you think that she knows, it does not hurt to reinforce it. It is good to hear those four words, if not often, but at least once in a while. It does not cost you anything, but it can save you a lifetime of headaches. Just tell her, "I love you, honey." Especially; if there are children involved. They, too, need the reassurance of their parents' love one for the other.

Storge is the natural affection shared with family members. Nevertheless, some boundaries must not be crossed for it to be a healthy family relationship. Many have crossed the line and ended up hurting many family members in the process. This is where incest happens. Many have been sexually assaulted by family members, and they blame God for what happened to them. This is especially devastating when they have been molested by the father in the family because then they want to stay away from Father God because of what happened to them. The one person who was responsible for protecting them was the one who violated them, leaving them vulnerable, and even hating their Heavenly Father in the process. They have problems receiving the Father's agape love because of what they suffered at the hands of their earthly fathers. I am so sorry you had to go through that painful experience, but don't turn your back on your deliverer. He can heal you and set you free. Father God loves you. The one who violated you was a selfish person, who, perhaps, had the same thing happen to him or her. And I say *her* because some women have abused their children as well. I say to those of you who are on either side to repent and ask God to forgive you, and believe me, He will forgive you and set you free from all unrighteousness. You can be made free today, if only you confess to Father God. He will deliver you and heal you even as you read this. Selfish people never think of the consequences of their actions. Better yet, people who are in bondage don't think twice about enslaving others. That is all they know. Some even think there is nothing wrong with what they are doing or have done. They are warped and have perverted minds. You must forgive yourself for you to be completely free.

The last type of love that I will discuss is philautia, which is the love of self. This love can be positive, or it can be negative. There must be a balance in everything, including self-love. Once a person goes overboard with this type of love, they become selfish and egoistic, and some are even narcissistic. Their view of things is distorted, but they cannot see it, and sometimes there is no reasoning with this person. They are myopic, and boundaries do not exist for them, and when called on their trespassing, they become vicious. At times, it is as if they are under a spell or controlled by the evil spirit of witchcraft. Thank God, Jesus came to give life and life more abundantly because God's love does not want, nor does it let us continue living in sin unless we desire to live outside the boundaries of His agape love. God is love and His love is yours for the receiving. So, open your arms wide and receive your Heavenly Father's unconditional love.

Reflection
God Cannot Stop Loving His People

1. Who is God?
2. What is one thing that God did to show His extravagant love for us?
3. Explain extravagant love.
4. According to John 14:6, who does Jesus say He is?
5. Is there more than one way to go to the Father? Yes or No. Explain.
6. What is pride and where does it come?
7. Who is the enemy of our soul?
8. Define agape love.
9. Identify and define each type of love addressed in this chapter.
10. What is the difference between like and love, and when should we use them?
11. Eros and Cupid are one and the same. What are they?
12. What must one do when under the influence of Cupid or Eros?
13. Why do some fall prey to evil spirits in their dreams?

14. What is a familiar spirit?
15. Name a great damage done by the misuse of storge love.

Chapter 7

God Cannot Tolerate Sin

Why do you think God turned His back on Jesus-His beloved Son on the Cross?

Jesus was carrying the sins of the world and God could not look at Him, because He is a Holy God, and He could not and cannot look at sin. A Holy God is who our God is, and because He is Divine, He cannot tolerate sin. If He could, there wouldn't be any need for the blood sacrifice of animals. There wouldn't be the need for the Lamb of God-Jesus Christ to lay down His life for us. The blood of animals was just pointing out to the Blood of our Lord and Savior. Animals' blood could only cover sin, and appease God for a season, and there had to be sacrifices often. But Jesus' blood was shed once and for all. The Blood of Jesus was and is incorruptible, and it is as fresh today, as it was the day Jesus shed it on Calvary's Cross for us. And, it will continue to be fresh forever. *"Forasmuch as ye know that ye were not redeemed with corruptible things, as silver and gold...But with the precious blood of Christ, as of a lamb without blemish and without spot" (I Pet. 1:18-19 KJV)*. His Blood is as powerful today and it was then, and it will continue to be powerful throughout eternity. It will never lose its power! Let me talk to you a little bit about the Blood.

When Adam was created by God, God put the breath of life into Adam, and in Leviticus chapter seventeen, we read that life is in the blood. *"For the life of the flesh is in the blood: and I have given it to you upon the altar to make atonement for your souls: for it is the blood that maketh an atonement for the soul" (Lev. 17:11 KJV);* thus, we are forbidden from eating blood-Old and New Testament-even before the Mosaic laws. God had spoken to Noah, and then later in the New Testament, the Apostle Paul tells us to abstain from meat sacrificed to idols and from eating blood. Why is this so important? God gave life to man. From His mouth to Adam's nostrils, He put blood into Adam's veins-life. Everyone walking around the earth has blood running through their veins, and without blood, they are just corpses. After Adam sinned, his blood became corrupted. However, Jesus' blood, because of the nature of His birth, was incorruptible, and that is why Jesus' body could stay intact for three days without decaying. Let me explain. Jesus was born of a virgin-Virgin Mary. Mary, the mother, provided the flesh side of Jesus-unto us a child is born, and the Holy Spirit, the Father, provided the spiritual side of Jesus-unto us a Son is given. Per medical research, studies have proven that the blood of a baby only comes from the father. The mother's blood and the baby's blood do not mix nor mingle during pregnancy. The blood comes strictly from the father. Thus, Jesus' blood comes from the Holy Spirit, making it holy. This is the reason why Jesus was the perfect sacrifice for our sin. He was and is holy because He carried in His veins pure and holy blood. His blood could not be corrupted because of its purity. Only Jesus' pure and holy blood could and can satisfy a holy God. It is because of Jesus' sacrificial blood that we can come boldly to the Throne of Grace, and we are not consumed. Remember, the priests in the Old Testament had to purify themselves before going into the Holy of Holies. Otherwise, they would drop dead in front of our Holy God. They had to wrap a rope around their ankles and have bells on their feet, so when they moved, the bells were heard (*Exodus chapters 28-35*).

Otherwise, they would have to pull them out because they were dead. Any little thing out of order or sin would cost their lives. Thank God for His grace and mercy. Thank Jesus for His sacrificial blood and thank the Holy Spirit for His involvement in Jesus' conception. We do well if we approach the Throne of God covered in the blood of Jesus. Without the Blood, we would be like the Old Testament priests. Aaron's sons, Nadab and Abihu, tried to offer strange fire to God, and looking at what happened, they dropped dead. Praise Jesus for His mighty blood. Please apply the blood of Jesus to your life *"And Nadab and Abihu, the sons of Aaron, took either of them his censer, and put fire therein, and put incense thereon, and offered strange fire before the Lord, which he commanded them not. And there went out fire from the Lord, and devoured them, and they died before the Lord"* (Lev. 10:1-2 KJV). Be cleaned from all your unrighteousness before approaching the throne of God. It is the Blood and only the Blood that gives us access to heaven and God's response. Apply the Blood. It is at the altar of heaven, the Mercy Seat crying out, "I paid for it." the Blood paid for whatever it is that we are asking the Father for in Jesus' name. It is the Blood that keeps us in the presence of a Holy God. Sin separates us, but the blood of Christ unites us back to the Father. *"But when this priest had offered for all time one sacrifice for sins, he sat down at the right hand of God, and since that time he waits for his enemies to be made his footstool. For by one sacrifice he has made perfect forever those who are being made holy"* (Heb. 10:12-14 KJV). Jesus is the High Priest of the new covenant. As seen in the Scripture, Jesus lives to intercede for us. He is the only sacrifice God would accept for our sin. Thank God for Jesus; otherwise, we would all drop dead before the Holy God. Our sinful selves could not enter His presence, and if we tried, we would all end up like Aaron's sons. Hallelujah to the blood of the Lamb of God, Jesus Christ, who is Lord and Savior.

Reflection
God Cannot Tolerate Sin

1. Explain why God turned His back on Jesus at the Cross of Calvary.
2. Explain why the blood of Jesus cannot lose its power.
3. Why are we forbidden from eating blood?
4. Why was the blood of Adam corrupted?
5. Explain the death of Nadab and Abihu.
6. Explain who is the new covenant High Priest and tell what He presented to God that gives us confident access to the Father.

Chapter 8

God Cannot Hate a Broken and Contrite Heart

Previously, I spoke about God's love. God is not asking you to come to Him perfectly. He is asking you to come to Him with a broken and repentant heart. The Bible tells us that if we confess our sins, God is faithful to forgive us and to cleanse us from our sinful deeds. *"If we confess our sins, he is faithful and just to forgive us our sins, and to cleanse us from all unrighteousness" (I John 1:9 KJV)*. Who wouldn't want to serve a God like this? *"For I will be merciful to their unrighteousness, and their sins and their iniquities will I remember no more." He will turn again, he will have compassion upon us; he will subdue our iniquities; and thou wilt cast all their sins into the depths of the sea" (Heb. 8:12 KJV)*. God is merciful. His mercy is fresh and new every morning. *"It is of the LORD'S mercies that we are not consumed, because his compassions fail not. They are new every morning: great is thy faithfulness" (Lam. 3:22-23 KJV)*. God wants His people to seek Him in the spirit of truthfulness. As we seek Him with honest and sincere hearts, He will hear us, and He will forgive us of our sins, and heal our land, even the land of our hearts and lives. *"If my people, which are called by my name, shall humble themselves, and pray, and seek my face, and turn from their wicked ways; then will I hear from heaven, and will forgive their sin, and will heal their land. Now mine eyes shall be open, and mine ears attend unto the prayer* that is made *in this place" (II Chr. 7:14-15 KJV).*

Years ago, for some reason, I needed to hear a black minister preach. Up to that point, I had been affiliated with a predominantly White congregation. A Caucasian sister in Christ invited me to attend a predominantly Black church's evening service. I got excited, and I accepted the invitation without any hesitation. This was my chance to see an African American minister in action. To my surprise, the church had invited a Caucasian minister to preach. The man was monotone, and he did not preach the exciting message that baby Christians sometimes like to hear. At least, the baby Christian I was at the time; however, his message was powerful. Don't ask me what he preached on. All I remember is that he said we all would hear that message twice; once that night, and then we would hear it again in heaven. He made an altar call, and the altar was packed. There seemed to be no room, but the saints squeezed in together at the altar. He prayed what seemed to be a simple prayer. But let me tell you, it was one of the most effective prayers that I have ever heard and experienced. My sister and I repented and cried for days. I repented of things I didn't even know what they were that I was repenting from and for. The message left an impression on me that I will never forget. I had experienced repentance under the anointing of the Holy Spirit for the first time. To this day, I am so very careful to walk with the Spirit of God. I do not want to do anything that I might not get His anointing to repent. I do know that God is a forgiving God, and He does right by His people because He is a merciful and gracious God. His grace is powerful; it gets us set free from bondage. I am so glad I am free. For whom the Son makes free, is free indeed. *"If the Son therefore shall make you free, ye shall be free indeed" (John 8:36 KJV).*

God taught me a further lesson that evening. I should not pre-judge His servants, His messengers. It is not about the messenger, it is about His message, and I do well not to look at the vessel being used for His glory. I am sure my first repentance was about my looking for the message to come forth through my mind's eyes, and not God's heart. I do know that I asked for forgiveness, and I am forgiven and made free from the deception of the enemy of my soul-Satan himself. I dare not tell God who to use nor how and when to use them. I am free, praise be to God, the Father of mercy.

One of the characters in the Bible that I look to quite often is King David. He had a repentant heart. He knew that when he sinned, it was against God first, and then himself, and lastly men. He did do some awful things, but he was always quick to repent. He wrote some of the most powerful prayers, and the amazing thing is, God never rejected him. Of course, there were some consequences to his actions, but God always restored him, and from his family line, we get our Lord and Savior, Jesus Christ, our intercessor, which clearly shows that God does not despise a regretful heart.

Reflection
God Cannot Hate a Broken and Contrite Heart

1. How does God ask you to come to Him?
2. What is God faithful to do when you open your mouth and confess your sins?
3. Explain repentance under the anointing of the Holy Spirit.
4. What is your take on the author's need to hear an African American preacher in the early stage of her Christian walk?
5. Thoughtfully, explain God's mercy.
6. Share a time God set you free, and tell how you benefited from your freedom and liberty.
7. Why does the author look at King David's heart?

Chapter 9

God Cannot Be Pleased without Faith

"*And without faith it is impossible to please God, because anyone who comes to him must believe that he exists and that he rewards those who earnestly seek him*" (Heb. 11:6 KJV). The greatest problem some people have coming to God is their lack of faith, and the Bible addresses those people as fools. "*The fool hath said in his heart, 'There is no God.' Corrupt are they and have done abominable iniquity: there is none that doeth good*" (Ps. 53:1 KJV). The hardest person to believe in God is the intellect. One would think that because you are an intellect, you should be the one leading in faith because you should be able to put two and two together. No, not so. The intellect sets out to prove those who believe in God that He doesn't exist. In his research and studies, he ends up discovering, that in fact, he is the one in the wrong. Therefore, he should let his spirit lead him, instead of his mind. His mind can only be good when it is connected to the mind of Christ, and the mind of Christ is operating through him because God loves those who come to Him in faith. "*Let this mind be in you, which was also in Christ Jesus*" (Phil. 2:5 KJV). The Word of God declares that He loves those who love Him and seek after Him early in the morning; those who put Him first in their lives daily. Yes, He loves those who are obedient to His Word and His Voice. *"I love them that love me; and those that seek me early shall find me" (Prov. 8:17 KJV).* You cannot love someone you do not believe exists. God has given us plenty of evidence of His existence. All you must do is look at nature. Night and day, summer and winter, the trees and the birds of the air, for they speak of the work of God. One must question who created the heavens and the earth. Can these be without the Creator? I think not. *"The fool hath said in his heart, There is no God. They are corrupt, they have done abominable works, there is none that doeth good" (Ps. 14:1 KJV).* Only a fool says that there is no God. Are you a fool? I think not. Therefore, put your faith in God. The Bible declares that God has given us a measure of faith. What is that measure? You decide! *"For I say, through the grace given unto me, to every man that is among you, not to think of himself more highly than he ought to think; but to think soberly, according to as God hath dealt to every man the measure of faith" (Rom. 12:3 KJV).* And because God has given us a measure of faith, we will have no excuses when we stand before Him on Judgment Day. The question should not be: "Does God exist?" rather, "What will happen to me if I chose not to believe His existence?" Well, the Bible is clear on that topic as well. You will have no part in Him; thus, your eternal life becomes eternal damnation, which is the state of being condemned to eternal punishment in hell. Let me remind you that hell was not created for you and me. It was created for Satan and his demons. They know God is real, why don't you? They deceive many into believing that God does not exist while they know He does, so they can have more residents of hell. Eternal fire is not a joke. Stay away from there, believe in God and His Son, Jesus Christ. *"If you declare with your mouth Jesus is Lord, and believe in your heart that God raised him from the dead, you will be saved. For it is with your heart that you believe and are justified, and it is with your mouth that you profess your faith and are saved. Anyone who believes in him will never be put to shame" (Rom. 10:9-11 KJV).* Trust in God and trust in His Word, and you will be saved now and throughout eternity.

Look at what Jesus said: *"Not everyone that saith unto me, Lord, Lord, shall enter into the kingdom of heaven; but he that doeth the will of my Father which is in heaven" (Matt. 7:21 KJV).* How can you do the will of Father God if you do not believe that He exists? To enter the kingdom of God, you must believe that He is and then do His will here on earth. He is not saying that you work for salvation. No, Jesus is saying that you must be of one spirit, one accord in agreement with God and His Word. This requires believing that He is. So, exercise the measure of faith given to you by God, and believe. It is that simple. The only one who has something to gain by unbelief is Satan himself. He has outfoxed many intellectuals with unbelief. Thus, he makes himself to be smarter than man created in God's image. *"And God said, Let us make man in our image, after our likeness: and let them have dominion over the fish of the sea, and over the fowl of the air, and over the cattle, and over all the earth, and over every creeping thing that creepeth upon the earth" (Gen. 1:26 KJV).* Let's look at the encounter Jesus had with the demoniac.

There was a man from the country of the Gadarenes who was possessed with demons, as you can see in the Scriptures, and he had been living in the cemetery. He was very violent and could not be tamed. He did all kinds of harm to himself. One day, Jesus came to his countryside, and when he saw Jesus from far off, he ran and worshiped Him. The next thing he did was cry out Jesus' identity. The demon said, "What do we have to do with you, Jesus the Son of the most-high God?" The demon recognized Jesus, the Son of God, and begged Jesus not to torment them before their time. Nevertheless, after Jesus asked him what its name was, he said, "Legion, for we are many." Jesus commanded them to come out of the man. The demons had to obey. We see that they tell Jesus their name. Legion was it, for they were many; approximately six thousand demons. The next thing it does is ask Jesus not to send them out of the region, but to send them into the herd of pigs that was on the mountainside. Jesus sent them there, and we see that the pigs could not tolerate them, and rather than live with demons, they chose to die by drowning in the sea. Demons are spirits, and spirits do not die. They did not die with the pigs. Later, the people of the region ask Jesus to leave their area. Why? Instead of the demoniac or the pigs, they were the ones possessed with the legion of demons. Demons, as you can see, recognized and obeyed Jesus. They know that God and Jesus are real. After all, God created them. Why do men believe the lie that Satan and demons do not exist? Or even that God does not love them. Do you not see how Jesus came for one possessed man and set him free? The people of the Gadarenes region could have been free as well, but they chose to carry demons instead of receiving deliverance and love from Jesus. *"And they came over unto the other side of the sea, into the country of the Gadarenes. And when he was come out of the ship, immediately there met him out of the tombs a man with an unclean spirit, Who had his dwelling among the tombs; and no man could bind him, no, not with chains: Because that he had been often bound with fetters and chains, and the chains had been plucked asunder by him, and the fetters broken in pieces: neither could any man tame him. And always, night and day, he was in the mountains, and in the tombs, crying, and cutting himself with stones. But when he saw Jesus afar off, he ran and worshipped him, And cried with a loud voice, and said, What have I to do with thee, Jesus, thou Son of the most high God? I adjure thee by God, that thou torment me not. For he said unto him, Come out of the man, thou unclean spirit. And he asked him, What is thy name? And he answered, saying, My name is Legion: for we are many. And he besought him much that he would not send them away out of the country. Now there was there nigh unto the mountains a great herd of swine feeding. And all the devils besought him, saying, Send us into the swine, that we may enter into them. And forthwith Jesus gave them leave. And the unclean spirits went out, and entered into the swine: and the herd ran violently down a steep place into the sea, (they were about two thousand and were choked in the sea. And they that fed the swine fled, and told it in the city, and in the country. And they went out to see what it was that was done. And they come to Jesus, and see him that was possessed with the devil, and had the legion, sitting, and clothed, and in his right mind: and they were afraid. And they that saw it told them how it befell to him that was possessed with the devil, and also concerning the swine. And they began to pray him to depart out of their coasts"* (Mk. 5:1-18 KJV).

Reflection
God Cannot Be Pleased without Faith

1. Who has the right and authority to use the Word of God?
2. Where do all godly prayers begin?
3. Name a few Scriptures to back up your response to where all prayers begin.
4. What key word did Satan use against Adam and Eve to deceive them?
5. What is one takeaway from this chapter that you can apply immediately to your life?

Chapter 10

God's Authority and Power Cannot Be Stopped

When I look and meditate on these verses of Scripture, I am in awe. *"All who live on the earth are nothing compared to him. He does what he wishes with the heavenly armies and with those who live on earth. No one can hold back his power or say to him, 'What did you do?'" (Dan. 4:35 KJV)* God can do, as it has been established already, anything He wants. He is that majestic. When we look at ourselves, we see that we are but a vapor; here today and gone tomorrow. We need to realize that we are just passing through earth, and there is a much greater purpose than work, eat, and collecting things that we will not take with us when we depart from here. We must focus on Kingdom work. This awesome and powerful God chose to create us in His own image, and He gave us some assignments. We have dominion over everything on earth according to His purpose. *"And God said, 'Let us make man in our image, after our likeness: and let them have dominion over the fish of the sea, and over the fowl of the air, and over the cattle, and over all the earth, and over every creeping thing that creepeth upon the earth'" (Gen. 1:26 KJV).* Somehow, some of us have lost sight of what our purpose here on earth was ordained to be and have strayed from the responsibilities assigned to us by our Heavenly Father.

It is time we repent and ask Him to forgive us. We know He is faithful to do so. Then, we must forgive ourselves and focus on the ministry of the Lord. Jesus told us to go into all the nations of the world and proclaim the Good News. Have you been doing that, or have you been distracted by the cares of the world? God, help us!

At times, we look at those God is using in ministry, and we see the anointing of God working in their lives, and some of us covet it. We forget to stop and consider the sacrifices they have made and continue to make to have an intimate relationship with God necessary for His glory to flow through them. *"I know that thou canst do everything, and that no thought can be withholden from thee" (Job 42:2 KJV).* Job paid a price for this Scripture. We benefit from his sacrifice and must be grateful for it. In this verse, we see another awesome characteristic of God. Speaking of sacrifices, years ago, I went to hear a Messianic Jew preach at a nearby church. I had never been to this church. A Caucasian sister in Christ called me and asked me if I wanted to go with her. She said, "He is a prophet." I thought, an Israelite prophet? Hum...This should be interesting, to say the least. I agreed and went. He preached a good message, and then for the altar call, I thought, he will prophesy over us. Yea, I was a bit immature. So, what happened next was something I will never forget. He said, "Please, come to the altar and pray for yourself." I went to the altar expecting God to speak to me. Something seemed familiar. I said to myself, "The altar feels familiar." After I made this statement, what the Lord said to me shocked me. He said, "Yes. That is your problem; you are familiar with the altar. However, until you and the altar become one, I cannot use you." Before going to this church service, the Lord had asked me to pray. At the time, I did not know it would turn out to be intercessory prayer. I had been praying for hours at the time, and not just one day a week, but many. I would go to church and lock myself for four, five hours at the time. I thought I was okay with my prayer life, but how many times has the Lord corrected us and set us on the right path with Him? I spent months trying to understand that statement. I finally got it. Crucify your flesh daily and put yourself on the altar as a living sacrifice. Live a sacrificial life. Be the sacrifice if I wanted to see results in my prayers. I know Jesus paid the price, but Jesus said, *"Then said Jesus unto his disciples, If any man will come after me, let him deny himself, and take up his cross, and follow me" (Matt. 16:24 KJV)*. I am so glad God spoke to me that day in that fashion. The Bible says that those He loves, He corrects. *"For whom the LORD loveth he correcteth; even as a father the son in whom he delighteth" (Pro. 3:12 KJV)*.

"God is the one who gives us the gift of wisdom through His Holy Spirit. Still, it is a gift. He has all wisdom, and He is the all-wise God. "There is no wisdom nor understanding nor counsel against the LORD" (Pro. 21:30 KJV). What can we instruct Him in? Nothing! Sometimes men get in certain positions in life and become prideful and arrogant. If we could only see that they are gifts and talents God has given to us, we would not be so ignorant. Often, people look at me and have the wrong idea about what they perceive of being my accomplishments. I believe that God allows us to go through paths in our lives to equip us for our callings. I am fully fluent in four languages, and I speak a bit of the fifth. But the acquisition of these languages was not easy. I have also lived a disciplined life, with an attitude of study, to show yourself approved unto God. Many live in the same community, and they start elementary school and finish high school with the same classmates and friends. I did not have the privilege. I lived and studied in three different continents and four different countries. I did not have the continuity of friends as they did. I cannot relate to their childhood stories. Mine was different. What some do not know is that for many years, I felt that I was five different people. I did not feel whole. It wasn't until my late thirties that

I prayed and asked God to gather the scattered parts of me and to make me one, whole. All I wanted was to have Him unite the five me and make me one, whole. Jesus did it. He answered my desperate prayers because only He could make me whole, and I am so grateful for His love and mercy in my life. Now, I have peace within. I have shalom. My path was God-ordained as theirs were. There is no animosity. We all must walk the roads ordained by God for our individual lives. However, we need to see God in each other's lives, and we must appreciate and embrace our God-given paths.

God is great, and we cannot counsel Him, but He sure can counsel us. He did counsel and still counsels me. He taught me how to pray and collect all parts of me to become one within. In that, I also learned to come into agreement with God the Father, God the Son, and God the Holy Spirit. I couldn't be in one accord with the Holy Spirit in prayer if I were not complete. I was always looking for a place to belong, and I got hurt tremendously because I looked in all the wrong places. Attending a friend's church by invitation, I thought, I would be safe there, and I would fit in because of our friendship. She was my best friend, and this was her home church. She grew up in that church. One day while attending Sunday service, I was on my knees asking the Lord where I belonged. Only God and I knew my prayer request. He responded so fast. He said, "You belong at Jesus' feet and at my bosom." I was happy to hear that, but I said, "But Lord, I am still here on earth. I need a home church. Where do I belong here?" Silence! He did not respond, and He still has not responded to this day. I have settled it in my heart that I am peculiar, and I am not a citizen of earth, rather I am a citizen of heaven, and that is where I belong, even as my Father God said that day. I know there is no place higher and greater than at Jesus' feet, and that there is no place safer and holier than my Father's bosom.

Today, I rest assured that God has me in the palm of His hand, and no one can snatch me out from His mighty hands. Once things were settled in my heart, the Lord spoke to me one day on my way to work, and said, "You are an instrument of glory in my hands." I was puzzled by it. I thought, "What meanest thou, Lord?" I know I spoke to the Father in the King James Version. Well, He caught me by surprise. I was not expecting that. I was on the road, driving and just meditating on His goodness in my life. The prophet Isaiah states, *"Yea, before the day was I am he; and there is none that can deliver out of my hand: I will work, and who shall let it?" (Isa. 43:13 KJV)* I am glad that I am in His hands. Aren't you? Strong and mighty is He. No one is stronger, neither greater than our God, and His voice commands attention and obedience. People try to undermine God's authority, but that is to their bereavement. No one can overthrow nor take over His authority. It is best to do what God says to do. It is not wise to fight against God. He is merciful and patient. And because of this, some think that He is either weak, sleeping, or He cannot bring what He said to pass. Give it time, and you will find out that He is God and beside Him there is none. For your own sake, don't fight God, join in serving Him. *"But if it be of God, ye cannot overthrow it; lest haply ye be found even to fight against God" (Acts 5:39 KJV).* *"Do we provoke the Lord to jealousy? Are we stronger than he?" (I Cor.10:22 KJV)* I will continue talking about God's authority in the Mantle chapter, and you will see how amazing it is.

Reflection
God's Authority and Power Cannot Be Stopped

1. Who has dominion over the earth and what is the reason for this authority?
2. When we go astray, what must we do to be restored back to our Father God?
3. Explain why it is wrong to covet another's anointing.
4. Explain the statement, "Until you and the altar become one, I cannot use you."
5. Why does God allow us to walk in certain paths?
6. Have you ever felt that you were not whole? Yes. No. Explain.
7. Define *shalom*.
8. Explain: You belong at Jesus' feet and at the Father's bosom.
9. What does it mean to be an instrument of glory?
10. What is the end result of trying to undermine God's authority?

Chapter 11

The Word of God Is True, and It Is Truth

"*For with God nothing shall be impossible*" *(Lk. 1:37 KJV).* Engraving this Scripture in our knower, allows us to come to God with an attitude of respect and reverence, knowing that His Word is the absolute truth. Doubt and unbelief are sins. They cause us to disbelieve the Word of Truth and leave us with no way of escape. God is our source of life and reading and believing His Word propel us to an intimate relationship with the Father that can have no equal. The truth of the matter is that there is a Scripture in the Bible for every situation we may face. They are there for our benefit, but if we doubt the Word of Truth and doubt that the Word is true, we have no relief from our pain and suffering. God made it clear by leaving no room for doubt in who He is and what He is about. It is in the Bible, His Word, that we can get the information and knowledge. Knowledge is power. It is power that has been given to us by God. Well, I will exercise His power for good. Will you?

Many have been healed of awful diseases by believing what the Word of God says about sickness and disease. I remember years ago when my younger foster son was about three years old. He had asthma badly. I usually prayed every day after I fed the children their lunch. I would go up to my room for a minute. Little did I know that I would spend a long time in prayer and that it went by very fast; I would lose track of time. My children laughed one day when I told them that I would be back in a minute. They said, "Yea, hours." They knew I was praying. One fine day during prayer, the Lord gave me a vision of my three-year-old foster son being healed. I saw an eagle eating worms out of his belly. The interpretation was that he was healed from asthma. I said, "Praise the Lord for His healing power." I came downstairs and told my children the vision, and I told them, "The Lord wanted you to know, so when the healing is manifested in the natural, you will know that He did it." Sure enough, the enemy came to challenge God's healing provision for the child. He was hospitalized within a day of the vision, for five days and four nights. I held on to the vision. My children said, "Mommy, didn't you say that God healed him?" I said, "Yes. God has healed him. Just hold on, you will see the power of God manifested in his life." God did it. *"Therefore, I say unto you, What things so ever ye desire, when ye pray, believe that ye receive them, and ye shall have them" (Mk. 11:24 KJV).* It wasn't too long after that, about two weeks, that the full healing took place. He is thirty years old now and free from asthma. Some say he grew out of it. I say the devil is a liar and the father of the lie. God healed him. I thank Jesus, for He is the Healer, and the Word of Truth tells me that through a prophecy from the Old Testament. *"Surely he hath borne our griefs, and carried our sorrows: yet we did esteem him stricken, smitten of God, and afflicted. But He was wounded for our transgression, he was bruised for our iniquities; the chastisement of our peace was upon him; and with his stripes, we are healed" (Isa. 53:4-5 KJV).* And then in the New Testament, I see how Jesus did it by taking those awful lashes, even before He suffered the pain of the Cross. *"Who his own self bare our sins in His own body on the tree, that we, being dead to sins, should live unto righteousness: by whose stripes ye were healed" (I Pet. 2:24 KJV)*. Historians have proven that Jesus did exist and that He did suffer the death of the Cross. You believe them. Why not believe godly men inspired by God's Holy Spirit who wrote the Word as we have it today. Why not believe God? Can you argue and challenge someone's testimony of what God has done in their lives? I dare not. The Word works. I know because God said it, and because it has worked in the areas of my life that I have allowed it to operate. Early in my Christian walk, I had a dream. In the dream, I found myself face-to-face with Jesus. I knew I was going to die. I said to Jesus, "I have not completed my assignment here on earth. Please do not take me home early." Next, what I dreamed did happen. I was at a women's Aglow conference in Ocean City, Maryland. There was a storm. I did not realize how strong the wind was until I tried to cross between two buildings. The wind came at me with a mighty force. I could not handle it. It had me rolling down the hotel's parking lot, and there was nothing I could do about it. Soon it would have me on the road and God knows what else. I remember thinking about my dream and my conversation with Jesus. I remember that God is love, and He loves me. I said, "Lord, you will not let me die just because you love me." It was then that I saw a flimsy bush that looked like it was dead. I grabbed a hold of it as I was flying by. I gained my senses, and my faith was refreshed and renewed. I called on Jesus, and just then, it felt like a mighty strong hand had put me on solid ground, and I walked the rest of the way through the parking lot to the main hotel conference room as if the wind had subsided. I came out of it with scratches, bruises, and a concussion. What the enemy intended for evil, God turned for my good. I never take God's warning for granted. The Bible talks about dreams and visions. I believe His Word. If I did not, I would have been the one to miss out on what God had ordained for me. Today, I am an ordained minister of the Gospel of Jesus Christ. Satan wanted to take me out prematurely. But God! You see, after you have given your life to Jesus, Satan cannot have your salvation because Jesus is able and willing to keep those who entrust their lives to Him, and no one can snatch them out of His hands. What Satan is after is the ministry of Jesus in you. So, are you going to let him have your ministry? God forbid it!

"For I know the thoughts that I think toward you, saith the LORD, thoughts of peace, and not of evil, to give you an expected end" (Jer. 29:11 KJV). God has a plan for your life, and you must pay close attention to His Word if you are going to work in advancing His Kingdom here on earth. You cannot allow deception to rule. You must trust and obey the Word of Truth. As I read the Word of Truth, I am looking for the Holy Spirit, my teacher, to teach me new things, and to show me how to apply them to my daily life. Make sure you do the same. *"Howbeit when he, the Spirit of truth, is come, he will guide you into all truth: for he shall not speak of himself: but whatsoever he shall hear, that shall he speak: and he will shew you things to come" (John 16:13 KJV).* God has made a way for you to learn and to apply the Word of Truth. It is up to you to obey and benefit. He has not asked you to do it on your own. He has provided all the help you will ever need according to His Word. *"If so be that ye have heard Him, and have been taught by Him, as the truth is in Jesus" (Eph. 4:21 KJV).*

Reflection
The Word of God Is True, and It Is Truth

1. What does the Word of God propel in believers' lives?
2. According to Mark 11:24, what happens when we pray with faith?
3. Who is a liar and the father of lies?

4. What is his purpose for lying to us?
5. Cite at least two Scriptures we must believe and quote when praying for healing.
6. Elaborate on a time when Jesus did something miraculous in your life.
7. Why is Satan after your ministry?
8. Explain: You must trust and obey the Word of God.
9. How does God speak to you?
10. Who is the greatest teacher that ever lived and lives? Explain.
11. As a believer, the only choice you have is to obey. Explain.

Chapter 12

God Cannot Go Against Your Will

The Holy Spirit is a gentleman, and He will not force himself on you ever. He will not come against your will, even though sometimes your will is detrimental to your health and your eternal life. In my late thirties, I wanted another baby so badly. Most women go through a stage in their lives where they want to hold another baby, love and nurture this child so desperately, that we feel like we cannot breathe unless this baby is in our arms; it is an ache like no other. This was my season, and I desperately prayed, without my husband's knowledge of my prayer request to the Lord for three consecutive years, but no answer. I could not understand why my prayers were not being answered. One fine day as we were on the road to do some shopping, I asked my husband if he wanted another baby. Without any hesitation, he looked at me with his nonchalant attitude and said, "No, indeed." It had never occurred to me that he had some say in the matter; after all, we were married, our children were all teenagers, and he did not want to start over. I understood his point. Consequently, I said to him, "So you are the hindrance to my prayers." He reluctantly said, "I guess, we could have another child." Soon after, I conceived, but you know what? The pregnancy resulted in a miscarriage. There was some water on the floor at my school, and they had not put the *Caution* sign out. I did not see the wet floor, so I slipped and fell, and what a great fall it was, and a few days later, I lost the baby in the first trimester.

You see, we both got our prayers answered. He did not want a child, but I did. When he reluctantly agreed to have another child, he gave the Holy Spirit the right to grant the answer to my prayers, while also getting his as well. He did not want another child, he was just trying to please me. One beautiful thing happened though, a day before I lost the baby on my way to work, I prayed a prayer I had never prayed. I said to the Father in the name of Jesus, "I commit her spirit to you." I had prayed the committal prayer. I did not realize it until days after, but that prayer brought me comfort. I knew my baby was with the Father. It is tough to go through the grieving process of a miscarriage because it is a silent pain. Most do not even know you are going through it, while others do not believe you even lost a human being growing inside of you. Regardless of men's opinion or the outcome, this baby was a miracle of God, and God was always there, comforting me with the committal prayer. I knew where my baby was and is.

The Bible clearly states that we know to do good; therefore, we know the difference between good and evil, and decide what to do. Does this mean we are the ones doing what we want, good or evil? This shows the Holy Spirit will not force us to do what we do not want; rather, He allows us to make our own decisions. Otherwise, He would be no different than a controlling spirit, which is against His will. God does not violate His Word, it is only when we call on Him that He helps us. *"Therefore to him that knoweth to do good, and doeth it not, to him it is sin" (Ja. 4:17 KJV).* Although the pain of losing my baby was like no other pain, I see God's mercy in it. Today, as I look back into those painful days, I see the Father's love in receiving my baby at that stage. Our God is merciful like no other, and all He does is for our good. I learned that one should always have the prayer of agreement, especially when it involves the other person's will and life. God doesn't force His will on us, and neither should we try to enforce our desires on others.

There have been times that I have asked the Lord to take my will and bend it to His will, because His will is perfect. I feel like the Apostle Paul must have felt when he said, *"For that which I do I allow not: for what I would, that do I not; but what I hate, that do I" (Rom. 7:15 KJV)*. Just the other morning during Communion, I asked the Lord for direction publishing my first book, the *Voice in the Cup*, and clear as day, I heard the Holy Spirit softly say, "The only option you have is to obey." Eighteen years had passed since the Lord had given me the vision to write, and three other prophetic words had come forth from people who knew nothing about my walk with the Lord. He had spoken to me, and He had confirmed it. Granted, at first, I was not ready, but there is a season and a time for everything, and now was the time. The manuscript had been through the content review, and now it was up to me to move forward with it. Consequently, I knew that I had to go ahead and finish what I had started. The Lord pays for what He orders. The money came in and all the expenses were paid. One thing for sure, I still had to choose to obey or not. I could have been disobedient, but what good would that do me and those who have been blessed by reading the *Voice in the Cup*? God will not go against our will, but He does expect our obedience. Obedience is always better than sacrifice, and obedience pleases the Father, and I am about my Father's heart.

Reflection
God Cannot Go against Your Will

1. Can you pray your will on another's life? Does it work? Yes. No. Using Scriptures, defend your position.
2. Do we know to do good? Yes. No. Back up your position with Scriptures.

Chapter 13

The God of the Impossible

We look at things sometimes in a negative and unbelieving way. God is not pleased with this attitude. He wants us to know that nothing is impossible for Him to do. Not only did He create the heavens and the earth and all that is in them, but He also did some awesome miracles afterward, and He is still performing miracles today for those who believe. He never ceases to amaze me.

I love when the Lord reveals something to me in His Words. One beautiful evening as I was reading the Word, the Lord showed me something special. I was so impressed that He continued to show me more. The more He showed me, the more impressed I was. He started with Jairus' daughter. I had read this passage many times, but never really stopped to meditate on it, nor did I fully understand it. As the Holy Spirit began to teach me about this miracle, I was so in awe, so impressed, that He took me to the widow's son. I was flabbergasted. I was thinking "how awesome!". This guy has been dead for at least twenty-four hours. In my country, people must lay the dead to rest within twenty-four hours. Those who pass in the morning must be buried by the end of the day, sometime in the afternoon. And those who pass in the evening must be laid to rest the next day in the morning. Thinking about this, I thought, "Well, he had to have been dead for many hours." I was looking and seeing this miracle differently and more deeply. I was impressed, no doubt about it. Then, the Lord said to me, "You are impressed? Let me show you something even more amazing." He then took me to visit the tomb of Lazarus, Mary and Martha's brother. Lazarus had been dead for four days, and as the sister so put it, he must have been stinking badly by then. This did not stop Jesus from performing the miracle. Four days dead. "Wow, Lord," I said. He said to me again, "Are you impressed with this too? I said, "Of course, Lord. I am so amazed." The more amazed I was, the more He showed me. Next, He took me to the Valley of Dry Bones. I know it represented the army of Israel, but the Lord was showing me that nothing is impossible for Him to do. Amazed and excited as I was by now, I could not contain my excitement about what He was showing me. I became like a little girl in her daddy's presence. It reminded me of the little children on the school bus, as one says, "My dad can lift a car," and the other trying to outdo, would say, "My dad can lift a bus," and so on... The little girl in me was saying, "My daddy can raise the dead-fresh, stinking, or dry." It was at this moment that the Lord took me to the beginning of man-Adam. Not only could He raise the dead, no matter how long the person had been dead, but He could and did create man from dirt. My Father, as I saw and see it, was showing His little girl that He can do anything, and all you and I must do is have faith and believe Him and take Him at His Word. Often, He takes me to this Scripture: *"He that spared not his own Son, but delivered Him up for us all, how shall he not with him also freely give us all things?" (Rom. 8:32 KJV)* This Scripture is very powerful. I read it and I quote it at times so I can keep it fresh in my knower, and at other times, I quote it in prayer because I know that if He did not spare Jesus from the awful death-He died for you and me-He will not withhold any good thing from us. He offered Him up for us. Is there anything else He will not do for us? I think not! This Scripture is so important to know and believe when one is praying with the result and for the result. I cannot emphasize it enough. I love the way the Lord took me on an adventure throughout the Bible, beginning in the New Testament, and moving to the Old Testament. Each time, the miracle in man's eyes looked a little bit more challenging. Was He showing them to me because it was challenging to Him? NO! Nothing is difficult for Him, and nothing is impossible for Him. He wanted to spend quality time with His daughter. He wanted to teach His little girl about His power, and He wanted my faith in Him to increase. After all, He is the teacher, and teaching He did with me that day. I cannot help to feel His love for me in the progression of that teaching. I loved every moment of it. I love to travel, and I felt I was on a journey with my Daddy. I love educational tours and I have led many for high schoolers and parent chaperones. My Father God took me on an educational tour of the Bible that day, and the companies I have traveled with all over the continents had nothing on my Daddy. Why am I saying this? I want you to see that He is a personal God, and He is very interested in what interests you. He did put the desire in your heart, and He does know you well. He knows that I enjoy a vacation like most, but given the choice, I prefer an educational tour. This is not to say that I have not traveled abroad to teach and preach the gospel of Jesus Christ, which is my very best reason for traveling domestically and internationally. It is my passion to spread the Good News.

Our Father God is very interested in nurturing and developing that which He has placed in us for His glory. I cannot explain my heart's excitement when He shows me something in His Word, especially when He is teaching me about Him and who He is. My Daddy is the God of the impossible. If He said it, He will do it. Nothing is a challenge to Him and for Him. He created the heavens and the earth and everything in them, I am positively sure; He can move His creation around to do whatever He wants to be done. Believe Him, trust Him, and it will go well with you, always, no matter the outcome. In the end, it will be for your good. God has your past, present, and future in His loving and unchanging hands, and He will not withhold any good thing from you. *"For the LORD God is a sun and shield: the LORD will give grace and glory: no good thing will he withhold from them that walk uprightly"* (Ps. 84:11 KJV).

Reflection
The God of the Impossible

1. How does God view unbelief?
2. What is your takeaway on the author's journey through the Bible with her Heavenly Father?
3. How have you applied Romans 8:32 in your life?
4. Stop, meditate, and define your relationship with the Father.

Chapter 14

God Can Never Be Worshiped Too Much

W hen was the last time you lost sight of where you were because you were in the presence of the Lord and nothing else mattered?

First, we must define praise and worship, so we do not confuse the two. Praise is the expression of approval, honor, commendation, and/or admiration for a god, a ruler, or a hero. It is about what the person or God has done. There are different types of praise. One can praise God by spinning around under the influence of emotions. It can be done with instruments or with a spontaneous song and dancing. Standing with extended hands is another form of praise; physically kneeling or bowing as one gives God adoration through loud tone or shout, proclaiming with a loud voice what He has done, is another form of praise. We praise God just because He wants it. Worship, on the other hand, is different.

Worship is not about what God has done, rather it is about who He is. You pay homage, give reverent honor, and admire the God, who is your Creator, and the Creator of the universe. Worship is a lifestyle. God requires us to offer our lives, will, talents, and abilities to Him without any resistance, and all are tried by fire because worship must be pure and holy. We serve a holy

God, and to worship Him you have to live a consecrated life to God; that is a life kept from any form of idol worship. It demands the utmost loyalty, truthfulness, even suffering death rather than breaking the covenant, and you must make up your mind to serve Him, and you must know that you are sold out to God.

You can worship God in spirit and truth through Jesus Christ. It is the faith in the sacrificial Lamb, Jesus Christ, and His shed blood that allows you to enter the presence of the Holy God. This moment is a time to seek His face and not His hands. You do not come seeking anything other than spending intimate time with your Heavenly Father. It requires a humble heart, a consecrated life, and a reverential fear of the Most High God.

Knowing that Jesus is the one who gives you access to the Father causes you to have a self-awareness of respect, admiration, and awe for the Lord your God, and you understand and desire to be in His presence with astonishment, amazement, devotion, and adoration. This connection comes from an intimate relationship with God the Father because a pure and truthful heart and clean hands come in Jesus, your Lord and Savior.

Praise can get you to the Outer Courts, but worship brings you past the Holy Place and into the Holy of Holies, where the manifest presence of God dwells. Although praise is good, and God desires it, you must covet to become a worshiper of the living God. Many know how to praise, but they do not know how to enter into worship. You see a dog seeing a bone can wag its tail, and that can be considered praise; a tree branch can move with the wind, and that can be counted as a wave offering of praise. People are praised for some sort of accomplishment, but worship requires knowledge of the worshiped, dedication, admiration, and intimacy. You cannot worship Father God if you do not know Him. Hopefully, as you read some of the things He cannot do and why He cannot do them, gave you an idea of who He is, and how amazing He is. Also, when you look at who Jesus is and what He did for you so you can enter into the presence of God, and you meditate on His goodness, you can't help but worship Him. I often say that those who do not worship and must be propped and pried in a church service show where they are in their relationship or non-relationship with the Lord. They tell on themselves. First, they do not know the Father, the Son, and the Holy Spirit. They say that they have not even spoken to the Father in a while. They have a form of godliness. Because if you know the God who snatched you out of hell, and you know anything about hell, you will worship and worship as often as you can. Your life becomes a place of worship. The Bible says that your body is the Temple of the Holy Spirit. *"What? Know ye not that your body is the temple of the Holy Ghost which is in you, which ye have of God, and ye are not your own? For ye are bought with a price: therefore glorify God in your body, and in your spirit, which are God's?" (I Cor. 6:19-20 KJV)* And, if you are in fact the temple of the Holy Spirit, then you are a worship place. There must be worship in you, and you are not stingy with it. No one needs to tell you to worship. It is automatic. Worship is in you, and it is a part of you. Worship is not clapping hands, nor is it shouting or doing the "Charismatic jig." It is a heart sold out to God because of who He is, and in your worship of Him there cannot be compromises. Worship begins with a pure heart and clean hands. You must repent before the Father from all of your sins, and that is daily, giving no room for the devil to work against you so that nothing hinders your fellowship with your Lord, Jesus Christ.

Often, I lose sight of my earthly environment. I am so deep in worship and awe in the presence of my Father that nothing else matters. There are no distractions. I remember being at a worship service, and I entered in quickly with singing because I worship all week long. The singing portion of the worship service stopped, and the pastor as I learned later, had moved on with the service, but I was still in worship. I knew nothing of what was going on in the service. Truth be known, I was not there. My body was, but my spirit was in the presence of Almighty God, and I know you are saying about now that the spirit of the prophet is subject to the prophet, but haven't you ever been so lost in the Lord that nothing else matters? That is where I was this particular time. I was just sold out to Him at that moment, and nothing else mattered. That is where I went one could say, "wrong." Therefore, my daughter had to jerk me to sit down because I was being rebuked by the visiting minister. Later, I apologized to the pastor of the house. I meant no disrespect. Other times, I will be in the service, and I normally worship with my eyes closed to keep the distraction from interrupting my time with the Lord. The service will start with a few people, by the time I open my eyes, the church is full, and I have no idea when the people arrived. Other times, I have started to worship while driving, and I do not know how I got to my destination. My best place of worship is at home, because I do not have to be concerned with protocols. I remember one time my pastor asked me to lead in worship. I came to with him going, "Piz, Piz, Piz." I had told him that I am not good at leading in worship because I get lost in worship quickly, but he insisted, so I obeyed; but he found out that that type of leading in worship was not my forte. Other times, I have problems moving on with the service because the presence of the Holy Spirit is so sweet, and I do not want to move from that special place in God.

Recently, I had a vision while praying at home. The vision was that of a man in filthy rags. Before this man could enter the presence of God, he had to remove all the rags. Where God is, is holy, and no unholy thing can enter. The blood of Jesus purchased you the passage to the Holy of Holies, but there are some things you must do because you have your preparation part in worship. As a young believer in the Lord, I was at the point of entering in the Father's presence, but I had believed some erroneous teaching that stated that if I entered the presence of God, I would drop dead immediately. The teacher had not told me that the Blood grants me access to intimate relationships with my Father God. I got scared, and cowardly took steps back from the portal to His presence. I held back out of ignorance. But thank God for the blood of Jesus. Like the man in the vision, you too can remove your filthy rags and enter into His presence. All you must do is ask the Father to forgive you of whatever is keeping you from intimacy with Him. There are many things set to hinder our pure and holy worship, but the Father wants us to drop them off at the Outer Courts and never pick them up again. We may need to be delivered from some things, and deliverance is good. It is amazing to be made free, so we can worship our Father in spirit and truth. *"But the hour cometh, and now is, when the true worshippers shall worship the Father in spirit and in truth: for the Father seeketh such to worship him. God is a Spirit: and they that worship him must worship him in spirit and in truth"* (John 4:23-25 KJV).

"And being in Bethany in the house of Simon the leper, as he sat at meat, there came a woman having an alabaster box of ointment of spikenard very precious; and she brakes the box and poured it on his head" (Mk. 14:3 KJV). Don't be surprised if someone attacks you because your worship is extravagant, and worship must be extravagant. Just like God gave us the most extravagant gift, that of His Son, Jesus Christ, we must give back to Him our lives, holding back nothing. As a young Christian, I joined the singing and dancing worship teams. I worship with much love. Jesus not only saved me, but He also delivered me, and He healed me as well. I couldn't stop worshiping him. Today, as I have matured a little in the Lord, I worship Him for those reasons, but also because of who He is. Do you know your Jesus? Let me tell you a little bit about Jesus.

My Jesus is the King of kings and the Lord of lords. He is the amazing begotten Son of the Father. He is the First and the Last. He is the Amen. He is the Bright Morning Star and the One who holds the seven stars and the seven candlesticks. He is I Am and Emmanuel-God with us. He is the Lamb and the Lion, the Sacrifice and the High Priest, just to name a few. You can study the seven churches and see how He introduces Himself to the churches based on their need to know and honor Him. You, too, can worship Him based on where you know or need Him. I know Jesus very intimate as my savior, healer, deliverer, and provider. When I worship Him in those areas, it is not just because I read them in the Bible, but also because I know Him to be who He says in these areas of my life. It is not someone else's experience, these are my own experiences with Him.

Jesus, my Savior, took me and brought me from the kingdom of darkness, and He brought me to His marvelous kingdom of light. He snatched me from hell- a place where the fire cannot be quenched, and worms cannot die; worse yet, where God's presence cannot be because God is Holy. *"And they shall go forth and look upon the carcasses of the men that have transgressed against me: for their worm shall not die, neither shall their fire be quenched, and they shall be an abhorring unto all flesh"* (Isa. 66:24 KJV). Jesus is my healer. He has healed me from several diseases. I had four accidents within five years, and all four left me with a shifted brain and body out of alignment. Just as I was healed from one injury, I had another accident. However, each time, the Lord healed me from the brain shift and physical illness. Also, He healed me from an incurable disease. He is my Healer. This I know, because I read it in His Word and believed. Besides, He is the deliverer according to His Word, but He is my deliverer because He delivered me from the spirits of rejection, lust, and suicide. Being physically abused leaves you vulnerable and open to demonic harassment.

You feel nobody cares about you, nor do they want you around them. Everything that comes out of your mouth is an insult to them, and at times they act as if you are not even present. They do not hear, nor do they see you. And molestation is no different. The spirit of lust is imparted to the innocent, whether they know it or not, leaving them accessible to future molestation and/or acting out. Depending on who molested you can determine the wrong feeling you have or think you have. I say think because the enemy plays with people's minds, causing them to even try to take their lives. They feel worthless and hopeless. Suicide is a spirit that came in through rejection and molestation. They work together against your spirit. You need to know and recognize the enemy of your soul. This lying spirit raises its ugly head and tells you that you are worthless, and if you believe the lie, you are hopeless and think you have no right to life. You must unmask its ugliness and lies. Tell it that you know that God loves you and is your deliverer. You must understand that the enemy came to steal, kill and destroy, but Jesus came to set the captives free; hence, you must choose to be set free. *"The thief cometh not, but for to steal, and to kill, and to destroy: I am come that they might have life, and that they might have it more abundantly" (John 10:10 KJV).* You must believe that God has a good plan for your life. *"For I know the thoughts that I think toward you, saith the Lord, thoughts of peace, and not of evil, to give you an expected end (Jer. 29:11 KJV).* This Scripture is not to tickle your ears, and it was not just for Jeremiah. It is for you and me.

I experience deliverance firsthand. Jesus is without a doubt my deliverer, and because of His delivering power, I vow to protect children from imposters. I am gifted in the area and can spot a predator from afar. Many children have been spared because of the gifting of discernment of spirits in my life. Spirits are thieves who try to rob us of the perfect peace, worship, and life in Christ, but Christ Jesus gives us abundant life. Additionally, Jesus is my provider, and from the moment that I came into the saving knowledge of Jesus Christ in my life, I have never gone hungry, nor has He left me begging for bread. I put my undivided trust in Him, and I say, like King David said, *"I have been young, and now am old; yet have I not seen the righteous forsaken, nor his seed begging bread"* (Ps. 37:25 KJV).

Yes, I have every reason to love and to worship Jesus. I love Him and worship Him every chance I get, because of who He is, and because of who He is in my life. I begin my mornings with, "I love you Daddy, I love you Jesus, and I love you Holy Spirit." I even blow some kisses at each one as part of my good morning. One morning after spending the night worshiping God with singing for many hours, before I could say my good morning to the triune Godhead, I heard with a strong, yet loving voice and very clear, "Shalom." Jesus beat me to the "good morning." I know some may think that this is strange, but what is strange is not hearing from your Father God who loves you very much because you have not dedicated the time due to Him. Worship is not only your privilege, but it is also your responsibility. You were created to worship, and there is nothing more important in this lifetime and the one to come than that of worshiping Him. Another thing that has been happening with me throughout my day is that of the sweet-smelling aroma of the Holy Spirit. It comes often and in many places. You see, I worship the Lord all day long. Every time I smell the presence of the Holy Spirit, I want and do take deep breaths, as to get more of Him in me. I want more of His presence, more of His love and power in me. I love my Daddy, and I love being in His presence. Don't you? Then, join me in worshiping our Heavenly Father in spirit and truth continuously.

Although we do not worship to be blessed, we are blessed in His presence because we choose to honor Him by putting away all that is false in our lives and before Him, and we give Him the undivided attention that is due unto Him. Abinadab sanctified his son Eleazar to keep the ark of the Lord, and his house was blessed. *"And the men of Kirjathjearim came, and fetched up the ark of the Lord, and brought it into the house of Abinadab in the hill, and sanctified Eleazar his son to keep the ark of the Lord. And it came to pass, while the ark abode in Kirjathjearim, that the time was long; for it was twenty years: and all the house of Israel lamented after the Lord. And Samuel spake unto all the house of Israel, saying, If ye do return unto the Lord with all your hearts, then put away the strange gods and Ashtaroth from among you, and prepare your hearts unto the Lord, and serve him only: and he will deliver you out of the hand of the Philistines" And the men of Kirjathjearim came, and fetched up the ark of the Lord, and brought it into the house of Abinadab in the hill, and sanctified Eleazar his son to keep the ark of the Lord"* (I Sam.7:1-3 KJV).

There are always blessings in the presence of the Lord for those who worship Him. However, if you do not worship and serve Him, you bring curses upon yourself and even your people, like the Philistines did. They had no right to the ark of the Lord or the presence of God because they were idol worshipers. They took the ark after the war with Israel, where approximately 30,000 Israelites were killed, but it did not go well for them. Many of the Philistines got sick and died, and even their god Dagon was having problems. It kept falling on its face. It had to worship God. The Bible says that every knee in heaven, on earth, and under the earth shall bow before the Name above all names, and that is the name of Jesus for God's glory.

"That at the name of Jesus every knee should bow, of things in heaven, and things in earth, and things under the earth; And that every tongue should confess that Jesus Christ is Lord, to the glory of God the Father (Phil. 2:10-11 KJV). So, blessings are for those who

worship Him and Him alone. No other gods can be in the mix. Again, I said we must have pure hearts and clean hands if we want pure and holy worship for the Most High and Most Holy God.

For the past three years, I have smelled the sweet fragrant aroma of the Holy Spirit. The scent comes and goes as it pleases. At first, I wasn't sure of the fragrance, but since then, I have come to learn that it has been the spices used to make the anointing oil: *"Take thou also unto thee principal spices, of pure myrrh five hundred [shekels], and of sweet cinnamon half so much, [even] two hundred and fifty [shekels], and of sweet calamus two hundred and fifty [shekels], And of cassia five hundred [shekels], after the shekel of the sanctuary, and of oil olive an hin: And thou shalt make it an oil of holy ointment, an ointment compound after the art of the apothecary: it shall be a holy anointing oil" (Ex. 30:23-25 KJV);* and the anointing oil is symbolic of the Holy Spirit. I believe this experience is because of my dedication and worship to my Father God. The first aroma I identified was the calamus, which smells like warm spicy wood. Every time I smell it, I want to take deep breaths. It is so beautiful. With it comes a sense of peace and love, and I always have such a grateful heart that I can't help but say to the Holy Spirit that I love Him, and I thank Him for His precious presence in my life. In the past two months, I have not worn any cologne, nor have I used deodorant. I have not needed either one. Not too long ago, a sister in Christ came into my classroom, and she said my room smelled beautiful, and she asked me what I had sprayed. I just said, "What you smelled is the Holy Spirit." Recently, my brother-in-law, after I touched his hand accidentally due to the physical emotional contact restriction, said to me, "One thing for sure, you smell good." I said to him, "Do you know what you smelled?" I said, "That is the Holy Spirit." You are wondering why I told them. Well, it is an aroma like no other, and those who have not experienced it before will be trying to identify it. There is nothing wrong with telling them that they are experiencing the presence of the Holy Spirit because the Lord does not open everybody's nostrils to sense and experience His presence in this fashion. They are blessed as I am to have this amazing experience with the Holy Spirit. You see, when you have been in deep worship, you enter into the presence of the Lord, and when you come out, you bring with you the sweet-smelling aroma of the Lord, and you smell just like Him, and that can attract or repulse those around you. the Apostle Paul tells us that to those who are being saved, the presence of God is a sweet-smelling aroma, but to those who are dying it is repulsive. *"Now thanks [be] unto God, which always causeth us to triumph in Christ, and maketh manifest the savour of his knowledge by us in every place. For we are unto God a sweet savour of Christ, in them that are saved, and in them that perish: To the one [we are] the savour of death unto death; and to the other the savour of life unto life. And who [is] sufficient for these things? For we are not as many, which corrupt the word of God; but as of sincerity, but as of God, speak we in Christ"* (2 Cor. 2:14-17 KJV).

This fragrance of the sweet aroma of the Holy Spirit has been so strong these days that at times the aroma has come out from inside of me. I had my mask on as I drove downtown alone, and I said to the Holy Spirit, "Wow! You are coming from within me now. How amazing, Lord." Yes, we are the temple of the Holy Spirit. *"Know ye not that ye are the temple of God, and that the Spirit of God dwelleth in you? If any man defiles the temple of God, he shall God destroy; for the temple of God is holy, which temple ye are"* (I Cor. 3:16-17 KJV). Keep in mind that all of these experiences are part of the living in the overflow of the Father's heart and love. Being in the presence of the Lord not only awards you revelation of who He is, but it also grants you a better understanding of who you are in Christ. The Holy Spirit is the only one who knows the deep thoughts of God concerning you, and He reveals them to you at the time of intimacy with the Lord. It affords you knowledge of the deep things God has written in His book in heaven concerning your expected end. No matter how you see it, you benefit immensely from being in His presence. The chamber of intimacy is revelatory, and that is another reason the Lord wants to be intimate with His children; here is this solemn place where we belong in Him.

Reflection
God Can Never Be Worshiped Too Much

1. In your own words, tell the difference between praise and worship.
2. How can you worship God in spirit and in truth, and who gives you access to true worship?
3. What must you have in Jesus to connect with the Father?
4. What causes you to enter into the Holy of Holies? And who is there?
5. What does the Bible say your body is?
6. Why do some people need to be propped and pried to enter into praise and worship?
7. Where, when, and why should you worship?
8. What is one thing that really makes Jesus happy, and why?
9. Who is God's most extravagant give to us?
10. Explain why worship is extravagant.
11. What area of your life do you worship Jesus best, and why?
12. Explain how some evil spirits operate in unsaved people.
13. Why is it vitally important to live demon free?
14. How do you begin your day in the Lord?
15. What were you created to do, and why do you worship God?
16. Why did the Philistines bring curses upon themselves by taking the ark of the covenant?

17. How must our hearts and hands be before God?
18. What is one symbol of the Holy Spirit mentioned in this chapter?
19. How are we savor of death unto death to a group and savor of life unto life to another group? Explain.
20. What must be in the temple of the Holy Spirit?

PART II

Know the Mantle of the Father's Heart Is for You

Chapter 15

Living in the Overflow of the Father's Heart

On a Tuesday night during a group Bible study at my home, the Holy Spirit stopped us in the middle of the lesson as He prompted me to pray out loud. There was an urgency to utter the words He was giving. They had to be said because there is power in the spoken Word, and these words had creative power. I knew that whatever He spoke through me at that precise moment would come to pass because it was initiated by Him. The prayer came with a vision, and the vision was that of an overflowing bank account. Now, I am not a financial type of teacher nor preacher. Our Bible study was not about finance, so it caught me by surprise; in fact, we were studying the blood of Jesus. One of the brothers was talking, and I interrupted him and asked him to pause on what he was saying because the Holy Spirit wanted us to pray right there and then. The anointing was so strong. I was convinced that the Holy Spirit was teaching us something new. We did pray immediately, and the prayer was very powerful. Soon after the prayer, the Holy Spirit started giving us Scriptures on the overflow. We were all excited because we knew it really wasn't just about our finances. The lesson that night took a different direction by the leading of the Holy Spirit.

Living in the overflow is a taste of heaven, and the Word of God says, *"And after this manner therefore pray ye; Our Father which art in heaven, Hallowed be Thy name. Thy kingdom come, thy will be done on earth as it is in heaven" (Matt. 6:9-10 KJV).* We can pray heaven here on earth for our benefit and for that of the world, and when I look at heaven, I do not see anything unholy. In the overflow, there are no fears, no torment, and no worries. There is no lack. They do not exist because they are a sin against our Father God, who is perfect love, and we know that perfect love casts out all fears. *"There is no fear in love; but perfect love casteth out fear: because fear hath torment. He that feareth is made perfect in love" (I John 4:18 KJV).* We know that the places we fear are the places where we are not trusting our Lord and Savior. When we find ourselves with fear and anxiety, we must stop and ask God to forgive us and to help us overcome the spirit of fear because it is an evil spirit. It tries to sit in the throne of our hearts and the seat of our mind, places belonging to God, and only God's in the believer's life. We must not allow it. So, take control of your life and call on the Holy Spirit of the living God to help you, so you can be free from it, and live in His overflow, where there are no needs, no wants, no ungodly desires; neither are there sicknesses and diseases, and most importantly, that is where the presence of the Lord is most radiantly in our lives.

In the overflow, death and Hades cannot exist because their power is destroyed in the believer's life. Here is where the benefits of the cross of Jesus Christ, our Lord and Savior, is activated mightily because we are happy, we are content, we are satisfied, and we are relaxed in the presence of our Lord, and we are at perfect peace with Him. We find that Jesus is our shalom as we rest perfectly in His presence. We see how much He has done for us and how wonderful He is to us. In the overflow, we put our trust in Him, and we believe His every Word. We do not doubt;

therefore, unbelief has no room to operate in us. It flees along with all its malicious intentions and devilish works, and because of our freedom in Christ, we can join King David in saying, *"The Lord is my Shepherd; I shall not want" (Ps. 23:1 KJV).* When you are living in the overflow, you have all your needs met, and wants don't exist because God has given you more than you can even imagine. King David knew this well, and he expressed it so beautifully. *"Thine eyes did see my substance, yet being unperfect; and in thy book all my members were written, which in continuance were fashioned, when as yet there was none of them. How precious also are thy thoughts unto me, O God! how great is the sum of them! If I should count them, they are more in number than the sand: when I awake, I am still with thee" (Ps. 139:16-18 KJV).* He knew that nothing about him was concealed from God. Furthermore, he knew that God's thought towards him were lovely, and that he could not count his blessing, for they were more than the non-count noun sand. Not only did King David recognize the presence of God in his life, but he also recognized and was grateful for the daily overflow of God's love and mercy. He was sold out to God, and when your heart is sold out to Jesus, you, too, can truly say, "Give me Jesus, nothing else matters." Your eyes are on Jesus because He is all that matters, and He is your heart's desire. All you long for is your shalom, the Prince of Peace. You experience joy because God Himself rejoices over you with exuberant dancing and singing, and with this kind of love and excitement, you rejoice with Him and in Him because you find that here is where you belong; dancing and singing with your Heavenly Father. *"The Lord thy God is in the midst of thee is mighty; he will safe, he will rejoice over thee with joy; he will rest in his love, he will joy over thee with singing" (Zeph.3:17 KJV).*

The Lord touched my heart with the overflow prayer, and as I meditated in His prayer words, all I could hear was, *O taste and see that the Lord is good.* I got super excited. *"O taste and see that the LORD is good: blessed is the man that trusteth in him" (Ps. 4:8 KJV).* I did, and I do taste and see that the Lord is God and He is good, and I am blessed by Him because I trust in Him and His Word. He cannot lie, as we have already seen in His Scriptures. Therefore, we hold on to His every Word, trusting and believing Him to do what He said He would do. God will do what you believe Him for, and you will see in some popular prayers and acts in the Bible.

The first Scripture the Lord gave me was the Scripture of the miracle of the five loaves and two fish, and He showed me how He fed the five thousand men plus women and children. Then, He showed me that the twelve full baskets of leftover pieces were the overflow. Not only did He feed so many with so little, but also, there were twelve full baskets left. *"When Jesus heard of it, he departed thence by ship into a desert place apart: and when the people had heard thereof, they followed him on foot out of the cities. And Jesus went forth, and saw a great multitude, and was moved with compassion toward them, and he healed their sick. And when it was evening, his disciples came to him, saying, This is a desert place, and the time is now past; send the multitude away, that they may go into the villages, and buy themselves victuals. But Jesus said unto them, They need not depart; give ye them to eat. And they say unto him, We have here but five loaves, and two fishes. He said, Bring them hither to me. And he commanded the multitude to sit down on the grass, and took the five loaves, and the two fishes, and looking up to heaven, he blessed, and brake, and gave the loaves to his disciples, and the disciples to the multitude. And they did all eat, and were filled: and they took up of the fragments that remained twelve baskets full. And they that had eaten were about five thousand men, beside women and children" (Matt. 14:13-21 KJV).* Another occasion was when Jesus fed the four thousand with the seven loaves and a few fish. He is the God of abundance. *"And his disciples say unto him, Whence should we have so much bread in the wilderness, as to fill so great a multitude? And Jesus saith unto them, How many loaves have ye? And they said, Seven, and a few little fishes. And he commanded the multitude to sit down on the ground. And he took the seven loaves and the fishes, and gave thanks, and brake them, and gave to his disciples, and the disciples to the multitude. And they did all eat and were filled: and they took up of the broken meat that was left seven baskets full. And they that did eat were four thousand men, beside women and children. And he sent away the multitude, and took ship, and came into the coasts of Magdala"* (Matt. 15:33-39 KJV).

Next, one of my sisters from Bible study called me with the widow's miracle when the prophet asked her if she had anything, but all she had was a jar of oil. By the instruction of the prophet, the widow used that one bottle of oil to fill as many bottles as she had. She then sold them, generating enough income for her to pay all her debt, and for her children and her to live for the rest of their lives. That is living on the overflow. There is plenty left after the bills have been paid. Amazing! *"Now there cried a certain woman of the wives of the sons of the prophets unto Elisha, saying, Thy servant my husband is dead; and thou knowest that thy servant did fear the Lord: and the creditor is come to take unto him my two sons to be bondmen. And Elisha said unto her, What shall I do for thee? tell me, what hast thou in the house? And she said, Thine handmaid hath not anything in the house, save a pot of oil. Then he said, Go, borrow thee vessels abroad of all thy neighbors, even empty vessels; borrow not a few. And when thou art come in, thou shalt shut the door upon thee and upon thy sons, and shalt pour out into all those vessels, and thou shalt set aside that which is full. So she went from him, and shut the door upon her and upon her sons, who brought the vessels to her; and she poured out.6 And it came to pass, when the vessels were full, that she said unto her son, Bring me yet a vessel. And he said unto her, "There is not a vessel more". And the oil stayed. 7 Then she came and told the man of God. And he said, Go, sell the oil, and pay thy debt, and live thou and thy children of the rest" (II Kgs. 4:1-7 KJV).*

Joshua is another example the Lord gave me about living in the overflow. Joshua's faith used in the battle against the Amorites gained him victory. It took him commanding the sun and the moon to stop from setting. *"Then spake Joshua to the Lord in the day when the Lord delivered up the Amorites before the children of Israel, and he said in the sight of Israel, Sun, stand thou still upon Gibeon; and thou, Moon, in the valley of Ajalon. And the sun stood still, and the moon stayed until the people had avenged themselves upon their enemies. Is not this written in the book of Jasher? So the sun stood still in the midst of heaven, and hasted not to go down about a whole day. And there was no day like that before it or after it that the Lord hearkened unto the voice of a man: for the Lord fought for Israel" (Jos. 10:13 KJV).*

How much faith did it take Joshua? No more faith than what you used in accepting Jesus as your Lord and Savior; just a measure of faith. However, one thing Joshua knew was that His God was great and mighty. Do you know that? Years ago, the Lord had me preach a message, and He told me to paint a picture and to paint it well. Now, I am not an artist. He wanted me to declare His might. He gave me an illustration of boxes. There were small boxes, medium size boxes, and large boxes. The message began with the question: How big is your God? The whole idea was that based on how big you see God is how great He will work in you. God cannot be boxed; however, your view of Him in you will determine what He will do for you and through you. On my way to work one morning, as is my practice, I was conversing with the Lord. He showed me how much my faith in Him had increased. I felt God very BIG in me. It was as if my stomach had enlarged, and there was a great space between where I was before and where I was that day. I know it is not by feeling, but by faith, but I felt like I had grown twice my belly size. I knew when I stopped and where He began. It was an amazing experience, and all I could do was cry. I thought I would have to pull over on the side of the road. Tears ran down my cheeks uncontrollably. It felt just miraculously good.

On another occasion, the Lord began to show me in the book of Isaiah how BIG HE is. *"Behold the nations are as a drop of a bucket, and are counted as the small dust of the balance; behold, he taketh up the isles as a very little thing" (Isa. 40:15 KJV).* I have traveled to many countries all over the continents. I know how fast the airplanes move and how far they can go. Some of the places that I have been, it took me 20 flying hours at great speed. When the Lord showed me that the nations of the world are like a drop in the bucket in comparison to Him, I was in awe. All I could say is, "God, you are BIG!" Another time, He showed me the nation of Venezuela in my hand as if my hand was His hand, and I couldn't even see it. It was as an unnoticeable speck of dust. Again, I said, "Wow! God, you are BIG!" You see, we serve the great, mighty, and eternal God who has no equal in wisdom, in knowledge, and power. I cannot even begin to imagine how AWESOME He is. I just get bits and pieces as He reveals Himself to me gradually because I know that I could never see Him in His fullest. As a baby Christian, I could not understand how the elders worship all day long throughout eternity. One day, I got a glimpse of it. They faithfully bow down and worship God continuously because every time they see Him, they see something new, something different, something amazing. Living in the overflow requires faithfulness to God and His Word, and there is always a reward because it always works. *"Bring ye all the tithes into the storehouse, that there may be meat in mine house, and prove me now herewith, saith the Lord of hosts, if I will not open you the windows of heaven, and pour you out a blessing, that there shall not be room enough to receive it"* *(Mal. 3:10 KJV)*. I am not one to preach or teach on firstfruits, tithes, and offerings. I just obey. However, the Lord spoke to me one day and told me that His people do not prosper the way He designed it because they always do the 66 percent. Either they give tithes and offerings, and neglect the firstfruits; fast and pray, coupled with praise, and neglect worship, or they believe in salvation and water baptism, but do not believe in the baptism in the Holy Spirit. They may give of their money, but do not give of their time, talents, and gifts. Giving back to God is in everything. It is not just about finances. It is in all you are and have within you to give. The Lord told me that we are short in our giving because it is always one-third missing. All these things are partially due to ignorance, disobedience, and/or the influence of the enemy. The overflow is a place of obedience. Do you want to have more than enough? Exercise the following Scripture, put it into practice, and you will not be disappointed because God always honors His Word. You must not be afraid of lack. *"Give, and it shall be given unto you; good measure, pressed down, and shaken together, and running over, shall men give into your bosom. For with the same measure that ye mete withal it shall be measured to you again"* (Lk. 6:38 KJV).

King Jehoshaphat could have chosen to fear the enemy; instead, he pleaded with his people to seek the Lord, and they defeated Moab and Ammon with fasting, prayer, praise, and worship (I King 20:1-30). He knew the power of fasting and prayer. He knew the power of praise and worship. Seeking the face of God and involving God in his affairs resulted in a great victory for the Israelites. You, too, can have great victories if you give the full 100 percent. Do not hold back on God if you want to live in the overflow. I tell you the truth, after the revelation of living in the overflow, all I could do was and is sing. *This song rings in my spirit as my victory song and it can be yours too.*

Reflection
Living in the Overflow of the Father's Heart

1. Define living in the overflow.
2. Give three Scriptures used to illustrate the overflow in the chapter.
3. What must you do when fear is present?
4. What cannot exist in the overflow?
5. How does God rejoice over you according to Zephaniah 3:17?
6. Name two miracles performed by Jesus using food.
7. According to Joshua 10:13, why is his prayer powerful?
8. Identify some areas where you experienced an increase of faith.
9. What does God say about Himself in Isaiah 40:15?
10. Why do the elders worship the Lord non-stop?
11. What are some requirements of living in the overflow of God's heart?

LIVING IN THE OVERFLOW SONG

"I am living in the overflow, the overflow in my Father's heart. I am living in the overflow, the overflow of my Father's love. O, I am living in the overflow, the overflow of Jesus' heart. I am living in the overflow, the overflow in my Jesus' love. It is in the overflow of the anointing of the Holy Spirit that I am living in the overflow, the overflow of my Savior's Blessings." I am swimming in the overflow of my Heavenly Daddy.

L iving in the overflow is for those who are obedient in Christ and are willing to exercise the authority in the mantle of Christ by hearing and receiving His spoken Word, and you must know that He always confirms His spoken Word through His written Word, and three or more Scriptures because Scriptures interpret Scriptures. The Bible says that by the witness of two or three witnesses a thing is established. *"This is the third time I am coming to you. In the mouth of two or three witnesses shall every word be established" (II Cor. 13:1 KJV).*

After I sang the overflow song, the Lord showed me the following Scriptures: *"And when they were come into the house, they saw the young child with Mary his mother, and fell, and worshipped him: and when they had opened their treasures, they presented unto him gifts; gold, and frankincense and myrrh" (Matt. 2:11 KJV).*

"The multitude of camels shall cover thee, the dromedaries of Midian and Ephah; all they from Sheba shall come: they shall bring gold and incense; and they shall shew forth the praises of the Lord" (Isa. 60:6 KJV). "The kings of Tarshish and of the isles shall bring presents: the kings of Sheba and Seba shall offer gifts" (Ps. 72:10 KJV). Now, the blessings of the Lord are not to be hoarded. They are not just for your benefit, they are to further God's kingdom

work even as His mantle is for His kingdom purpose. Let us continue with the overflow by looking at the dew of God.

Reflection
Living in the Overflow Song

1.   Identify an experience you had with God that produced something spectacular in your life.

ROCÍO DE DIOS – DEW OF GOD

Recently, the Lord gave me a dream, and the words that came were in Spanish, which is not my dream language, unless I am directly speaking to Hispanohablantes in the dream, so I knew He wanted my undivided attention. He said "Rocío." I woke up with that word, but went back to sleep, but not before asking the Holy Spirit not to let me forget the word. It seemed vitally important, but I was too exhausted and weak to write it down. So, as soon as I woke up again, He reminded me of the word, but this time, out of my spirit, I said, "rocío de Dios," which means the dew of God. The Lord wanted to further teach me about the overflow of the Father's heart. Of course, I researched Scriptures and listened to the Teacher -the Holy Spirit, very carefully. The discovery was amazing.

Throughout the research, I found that dew is very good.

The dew of God speaks of God's favor, blessings, prosperity, abundant life, long life, and resurrection life. We know that those who are saved are already favored by the Lord; nevertheless, come with me on a discovery journey by the leading of the Holy Spirit through some Old Testament Scriptures.

Jacob is blessed by his father Isaac, and Isaac used dew in his prayer as it is seen in Scriptures. He prays the dew of heaven on Jacob's life, which brings the fatness of the earth. This is the overflow of the land. Fatness represents the richness of the land because it is fertile, and dew causes it to abundantly produce more than one's needs and wants. *"And his father Isaac said unto him, Come near now, and kiss me, my son. And he came near, and kissed him: and he smelled the smell of his raiment, and blessed him, and said, See, the smell of my son is as the smell of a field which the Lord hath blessed: Therefore God give thee of the dew of heaven, and the fatness of the earth, and plenty of corn and wine: Let people serve thee, and nations bow down to thee: be lord over thy brethren, and let thy mother's sons bow down to thee: cursed be every one that curseth thee, and blessed be he that blesseth thee"* (Gen. 27:26-29 KJV).

Before Noah's flood, there was no rain. The land's vegetation got their water from dew, and we know that rain is good, but not always. Rain, although from God, is something that can be damaging at times. It is something that does not require much attention to know it is present; however, dew is something that one has to purposely experience. You must get up early in the morning if you want to benefit from it. Having eight daughters and no son, my mom used to say, "Ai, da mulher de meio día pa tarde," which means, "Beware of the afternoon woman." In other words, be careful of a lazy woman, and that was all she had to say to get us out of bed when we did not want to get up, especially so early in the morning. In the American culture, it is said, "The early bird catches the worms." However, God's Word says it best: *"I love them that love me; and those that seek me early shall find me"* (Prov. 8:17 KJV).

There are some benefits to getting up early in the morning and experiencing the dew of God, whether it is time spending in your prayer closet with Him or fellowshipping with the Lord outside as you get the fresh air that you intentionally desire and need. Hearing the voice of God early in the morning sets you up for a great day; a day that is ordered by the Lord. You stay focused on what is important, and you can recognize the enemy's trap, and you do not pay attention to his distractions. You know what to do, when to do it, and how to do it because you already have your mandate of the day by the Lord. In addition, dew has properties that are good for your health, which brings the long-life blessing. It rejuvenates your skin and even helps with kidney function. I like how Moses put it in the following Scriptures:

"Give ear, O ye heavens, and I will speak; and hear, O earth, the words of my mouth. My doctrine shall drop as the rain, my speech

shall distill as the dew, as the small rain upon the tender herb, and as the showers upon the grass: Because I will publish the name of the Lord: ascribe ye greatness unto our God" (De. 32:1-3 KJV). Moses commands the heavens and the earth to listen to his words. He speaks to the third heaven even as the Lord Jesus taught us to pray. Let it be done on earth as it is heaven. *"Thy kingdom come, Thy will be done on earth, as it is in heaven" Matt 6:10 KJV).* He speaks to the second heaven- that of the kingdom of Satan, which we see in the battle of the archangel Gabriel and the archangel Michael with the prince of the air, trying to get through to bring the answer to Daniel's prayer. *"Then said he unto me, Fear not, Daniel: for from the first day that thou didst set thine heart to understand, and to chasten thyself before thy God, thy words were heard, and I am come for thy words. But the prince of the kingdom of Persia withstood me one and twenty days: but, lo, Michael, one of the chief princes, came to help me; and I remained there with the kings of Persia" (Da. 10:12-13 KJV).* Then, Moses speaks to the first heaven, which is the sky as we know it. Furthermore, he speaks to the earth. Moses speaks to all creation and commands attention. He talks of his teaching dropping like rain, loud and clear, but his Word gentle like purifying dew. Why is this so? He is publishing or declaring the mighty name of the Lord, and he compels them to attribute greatness to our God. It is noticeable how Moses delivers this powerful message to the people, yet he is soft and gentle like dew. His message is that of love and peace. He reminds the people of all that the Lord had done for them and warns them of the consequences of their wrongdoings. Keeping God's Word always brings blessings and prosperity as disobeying God's Word brings dire consequences to one's life. Notwithstanding, when we listen to the Lord and do what He says without compromise, He opens our spiritual eyes to see the blessings He has bestowed upon us. The rocío de Dios dream is a gentle way of my Heavenly Daddy speaking and encouraging me as if He was watering the vision and prophetic word concerning the overflow of the Father's heart in my life and that of those who believe in the vision of the overflow because God is no respect of a person. What He does for one, He does for the other, if only we believe Him and take Him at His Word. *"Then Peter opened his mouth, and said, Of a truth I perceive that God is no respecter of persons" (Acts 10:34 JKV)*. Here, the Apostle Peter is talking about the baptism of the Holy Spirit. Now, if the Lord does not discriminate in giving of His Holy Spirit, how much more the additional blessings that He provided for us on the Cross of Calvary? So, receive the dew of God and live in the abundance of God's grace and mercy. Live in the prosperity of His love and provision.

Every time I think of this dream, I can't help but feel the love and peace of the Father as He is embracing me with His presence. This is an indescribable experience, and I pray you experience such visitations from our Holy Father and God through His eternal spirit- His precious Holy Spirit. And right here, right now, I just have to say, "I love you Holy Spirit," and if you could see my face at this moment, you would see the biggest smile ever even as I take deep breaths in Him. Have the faith of a child and do as my friend from Bible study did and does. He received the vision and prayer on the overflow, and as he tells it, he grabbed it, closed his hand, and put it in his pocket. Every time he thinks of it, he takes it out, looks at it, he thanks God for His overflow, and he puts it back in his pocket. He has been blessed more than he can ever remember, and he is seventy-five years old. You, too, can do the same. Operate on the faith of a mustard seed and that of a child. *"And Jesus said unto them, Because of your unbelief: for verily I say unto you, If ye have faith as a grain of mustard seed, ye shall say unto this mountain, Remove hence to yonder place; and it shall remove; and nothing shall be impossible unto you" (Matt. 17:20 KJV). "Verily I say unto you,*

Whosoever shall not receive the kingdom of God as a little child shall in no wise enter therein" (Lk. 18:1 KJV).

Needless to say, the blessings of the Lord are not to be hoarded. They are not just for your benefit; they are to further God's kingdom work even as His mantle is for His kingdom purpose. Consequently, we will examine some Old Testament mantles.

Reflection
Rocío de Dios – Dew of God

1. Define rocío de Dios or dew of God.
2. Name some benefits of the dew of God and tell how we should use these benefits.
3. What is the spiritual difference between dew and rain?
4. According to Proverbs 18:17, what does God say about those who seek Him early in the morning?
5. According to Deuteronomy 32:1-2, who does Moses speak to and what is the purpose of his speech?
6. Explain the difference between the three heavens.
7. What is the faith of a mustard seed?

Chapter 16

Old Testament Mantles

MANTLE OF WORSHIP, MOURNING, AND REPENTANCE

The mantle is used symbolically in the Bible as a righteous call and covering in the fulfillment of one's mandate by God; and in the Old Testament, there were various mantles and they had various uses, which I will discuss briefly so there is a better understanding of mantles. Thus, you will understand how important it is to select and carry the right mantle. This study will also help you comprehend the power and authority that is found in the mantle of the Father's heart. Let's look at how Job used his mantle on a sad occasion for a moment.

According to God, Job was a perfect, righteous man who feared the Lord, and there was no one like him on the face of the earth during his days. Now, Job's children were the opposite of their father. They lived unrighteous lives, and Satan used them against Job. The enemy always uses what is precious to torment us, and Job was no different, but Satan can only do to us what he is allowed by God even as it was with Job. God allowed him to take everything from Job, but his life. Job gets one bad news after the other, and Satan thought that Job would sin against God, but what does Job do? He rents his mantle, shaves his head, and falls to the ground in worship, and he said naked he had come from his mother's womb and naked he would leave this world. *"Then Job arose, and rent his mantle, and shaved his head, and fell upon the ground, and worshipped" (Job 1:20 KJV).* Later, we see Job's friends renting their mantles as a sign of mourning for the loss of their friend's children and possession. *"And when they lifted their eyes afar off and knew him not, they lifted their voice, and wept; and they rent everyone his mantle, and sprinkled dust upon their heads toward heaven" (Job 2:12 KJV).*

Ezra rents his mantle as a sign of sadness and repentance, and he gets on his knees and prays to the Lord. However, regardless of the devastating news, his posture is similar to that of Job. He fell upon his knees in prayer and worship. You see, God always receives worship from those who know him irrespective of the situation because they know that He is sovereign. *"And when I heard this thing, I rent my garment and my mantle, and plucked off the hair of my head and my beard, and sat down astonied. Then were assembled unto me every one that trembled at the words of the God of Israel, because of the transgression of those that had been carried away; and I sat astonied until the evening sacrifice. And at the evening sacrifice I arose up from my heaviness; and having rent my garment and my mantle, I fell upon my knees, and spread out my hands unto the Lord my God" (Ezr. 9:3-5 KJV).*

THE MANTLE OF DEATH

During Prophetess Deborah's time as the judge of Israel, the Israelites did evil in the sight of God, and God sold them into the hands of Jabin, the king of Canaan. However, after suffering for a while, the children of Israel cried out in repentance to God, and God had mercy upon them; and with God's help, they went to battle against the Canaanites. Prophetess Deborah knew that Israel was to fight for their freedom; so, she sent for Barak, the son of Abinoam, to lead the army of Israel. Barak agreed to go, but only if Prophetess Deborah went with him. She agrees, but under the understanding that God would deliver the army of Canaan to a woman. Barak consented to the terms and they went. Now, Sisera, the captain of the army of King Jabin, led the Canaanites into battle against Israel. Israel was winning the battle, sending Sisera cowardly running for his life into the tent of Jael. Jael was the wife of Heber, a Kenite woman, whose people supposedly were at peace with King Jabin; thus, Sisera had peace as well with the house of Heber; this caused him to be easily persuaded to turn into the tent of Jael for safety. Jael, upon the request of Sisera, gives him some milk to drink because he was thirsty. Not only was he thirsty, but he was also exhausted from the battle. He drinks the milk and then is covered with a mantle that Jael provided for his covering to hide him from the Israelites. Immediately, Sisera falls asleep, and Jael grabs a nail from her tent and smote the nail into his temples and kills him. Later, she presents Sisera dead to Barak, who had been in pursuit of Sisera. This mantle was the mantle of death. Sisera, although an evil man, let his guard down and wore the wrong mantle, which became his death covering in the hands of a woman. *"And Jael went out to meet Sisera, and said unto him, turn in, my lord, turn in to me; fear not. And when he had turned in unto her into the tent, she covered him with a mantle"* (*Jdg. 4:18 KJV*). As you can see from Sisera's account, some mantles bring judgment and death to those who wear them.

THE MANTLE OF JUDGMENT

King Saul, the first king of Israel, is rejected by the Lord as king of Israel because he rejected the voice of the Lord in utterly destroying all of the Amalekites as commanded. Furthermore, Saul showed favoritism, and we know that with God there is no respect of persons. God honors those who honor Him, and Saul dishonored Him by not obeying His command and doing what He told Saul to do. King Saul did partial obedience, and partial obedience is no obedience at all. He also feared men more than he reverenced God, and God will not allow anyone to put others before Him. In the first commandment, God tells us not to have any other gods before Him, and a god can be anything that is put before God. Saul asked the prophet Samuel to go with him, but he could not because he knew God had rejected Saul as king. The prophet was not going to go against God's voice. Although Samuel had mourned for King Saul a lot before God in the end, King Saul ripped the prophet Samuel's mantle, and that sealed the rejection of God towards King Saul. As Saul rented the prophet's mantle, so did God rent the kingdom of Israel from Saul. *"Wherefore then didst thou not obey the voice of the Lord, but didst fly upon the spoil and didst evil in the sight of the Lord? And Saul said unto Samuel, Yea, I have obeyed the voice of the Lord, and have gone the way which the Lord sent me, and have brought Agag the king of Amalek, and have utterly destroyed the Amalekites. But the people took of the spoil, sheep and oxen, the chief of the things which should have been utterly destroyed, to sacrifice unto the Lord thy God in Gilgal. And Samuel said, Hath the Lord as great delight in burnt offerings and sacrifices, as in obeying the voice of the Lord? Behold, to obey is better than sacrifice, and to hearken than the fat of rams. For rebellion is as the sin of witchcraft, and stubbornness is as iniquity and idolatry. Because thou hast rejected the word of the Lord, he hath also rejected thee from being king. And Saul said unto Samuel, I have sinned: for I have transgressed the commandment of the Lord, and thy words: because I feared the people, and obeyed their voice. Now, therefore, I pray thee, pardon my sin, and turn again with me, that I may worship the Lord. And Samuel said unto Saul, I will not return with thee: for thou hast rejected the word of the Lord, and the Lord hath rejected thee from being king over Israel. And as Samuel turned about to go away, he laid hold upon the skirt of his mantle, and it rent"* (I Sam. 15:9-27 KJV).

King Saul became so desperate to hear a word from God that he consults with the witch of Endor. He had gotten rid of all the witches in the land, but in his desperation, he seeks a witch to bring the spirit of the prophet Samuel from the dead to speak with him. *"And he said unto her, What form is he of? And she said An old man cometh up, and he is covered with a mantle. And Saul perceived that it was Samuel, and he stooped with his face to the ground and bowed himself"* (I Sam. 28:14 KJV). Now, this is totally against the Word and the will of God. King Saul does not get the prophet to speak to him, what he gets is a familiar spirit.

First of all, God was and is against witchcraft. Second, if Samuel refused to speak to Saul while he was alive, why would he speak to him after death. Also, the Bible says, "absent from the body, present with the Lord." In those days, the prophet would have been in Abraham's bosom until Jesus' visit. There was no need for King Saul to look for the anointing he had lost. God is not a man that He should repent. He knows what He does from the beginning to the end- He is the Alpha and the Omega. *"I am Alpha and Omega, the beginning and the ending, saith the Lord, which is, and which was, and which is to come, the Almighty"* (Rev. 1:8 KJV).

THE MANTLE OF REMOVAL

There is a time for everything, and the removal of mantles is no different. The prophet Isaiah prophesies to the daughters of Israel. In it, he tells them that God would strip them naked to the point where even their mantles or coverings were removed from them because they sinned against God. *"The bonnets, and the ornaments of the legs, and the headbands, and the tablets, and the earrings, The rings, and nose jewels, The changeable suits of apparel, and the mantles, and the wimples, and the crisping pins, The glasses, and the fine linen, and the hoods, and the vails. And it shall come to pass, that instead of sweet smell there shall be stink; and instead of a girdle a rent; and instead of well-set hair baldness; and instead of a stomacher a girding of sackcloth; and burning instead of beauty"* (Isa. 3:20-24 KJV).

The Transferring Mantle

The prophet Elijah, an Old Testament prophet, had the mantle of God, which he used with much power and authority to fulfill the calling of God in his life. Elijah is one of two people who do not die in the entire Bible, and it is believed that he will return as one of the two witnesses before the coming of Jesus, the Christ. *"And Elijah said unto Elisha, Tarry here, I pray thee; for the Lord hath sent me to Bethel. And Elisha said unto him, As the Lord liveth, and as thy soul liveth, I will not leave thee. So they went down to Bethel"* (2 Kin. 2:8 KJV). In the following Scriptures, we see Elijah's protégé, Elisha, receiving the mantle of Elijah. *"He took up also the mantle of Elijah that fell from him, and went back, and stood by the bank of Jordan; And he took the mantle of Elijah that fell from him, and smote the waters, and said, Where is the Lord God of Elijah? and when he also had smitten the waters, they parted hither and thither: and Elisha went over. And when the sons of the prophets which were to view at Jericho saw him, they said, The spirit of Elijah doth rest on Elisha. And they came to meet him and bowed themselves to the ground before him"* (2 Kin. 2:13-15 KJV). Immediately, Elisha puts the mantle to test. He wants to make sure he has received the authentic mantle of Elijah that came from the God of Elijah and his God. Later, we see that Elisha is elevated and validated by God as Elijah's successor when God parts the waters for him to cross over. Elisha had walked with Elijah, and he knew this was no ordinary mantle. He knew it was authentic and that Elijah carried the mantle of God because of his relationship with the Lord. He had accompanied Elijah, and he had witnessed many miracles during his service to Elijah. He, too, was authentic, and God knew his heart; thus, He granted the transferring of the mantle from Elijah to Elisha. Like Elisha, one must test the mantle before accepting and operating in it because not all mantles are equal. Elisha carried the mantle of glory and honor, but how many mantles are out there that are and do the opposite?

THE MANTLE OF CONFUSION

There is a mantle of confusion, and you do not want to operate in it. You must run from it and run as fast and as far as possible. *"Let mine adversaries be clothed with shame, and let them cover themselves with their confusion, as with a mantle" (Ps. 109:29 KJV).* In his prayer, King Davis asks God to let his adversaries be covered as with a mantle with the same confusion they wanted for him. In other words, let them be exposed and stripped naked from their mantles, naked in their folly. Having no secret devices against King David, instead of them being clothed with mantles of honor, let them be clothed with dishonor and confusion. All that they wished on King David, he asked God to return to them. You see, you can send back to the sender the ungodly things they wished and sent after you. King David did not play, nor did he entertain and romance the enemy. He was firm; he was clear and precise in making his requests known to God, and the desires of his heart were granted. At one time, these people may have worn mantles of honor, but somehow, they lost their way and they became dishonorable men who lost their glory. A mantle can carry honor or dishonor. It is up to the individuals which mantle they choose to carry. God always gives us the choice to choose between good and evil; to choose Him or Satan. The choice is always ours. Granted, this mantle is not that of God, but it was a covering, and we can choose to be covered with honor or with shame. In doing so, we must be very careful with who we associate with and allow their input in our lives. The mantle of confusion comes from the author of confusion, and that is Satan because God is the author of peace. *"For God is not the author of confusion, but of peace, as in all churches of the saints"* (I Cor. 14:33 KJV).

When we look at the Old Testament prophets, we see men who took their assignments from God very seriously. They did reverence God and served Him with fear and trembling, and because of that, God used them mightily. They knew the voice of God and they obeyed. They had an intimate relationship with the Lord, and because of that, they did not question whose voice had spoken to them. They knew even as Jesus said, *"My sheep hear my voice, and I know them, and they follow me: And I give unto them eternal life; and they shall never perish, neither shall any man pluck them out of my hand"* (John 10:27-28 KJV). Their callings were dramatic, leaving no room for doubt and unbelief. We see Moses and his experience with the burning bush (Exodus chapter 3). Isaiah had the vision of the Lord sitting upon His throne, high and lifted up; that is in Isaiah chapter 6. Jeremiah chapter one talks about Jeremiah's encounter with the Lord, and the Lord tells him that He had called him to be a prophet to the nations even before he was formed in his mother's womb. Then, Ezekiel talks about the vision of the living creatures and the wheels as God sends him to the children of Israel in Ezekiel chapters 1 and 2. All of them had dramatic encounters with the Lord at the beginning of their calling. We must know who called us and whose mantle we carry. It is vitally important to understand the mantle and its mandates; however, we cannot comprehend it without knowing our Heavenly Father intimately. In knowing Him, we can understand and discern the difference between the mantle of God and spiritual coverings.

Reflection
Old Testament Mantles

1. According to the Old Testament, define the word *mantle*.
2. What is a mantle of worship? How is the mantle of mourning described in this chapter?
3. Describe the mantle of repentance.
4. Who wore the mantle of death, and why?
5. Who prayed the mantle of judgment prayer, and why?
6. Who had their mantle removed, and why?
7. For what purpose was Elijah's mantle transferred to Elisha?
8. What is the mantle of confusion?
9. What is your greatest takeaway from this chapter?

Chapter 17

Coverings

What is a pastor's covering? It is the process of spiritual shielding, protecting, and providing true fathering or mothering and mentorship to individuals in the local church or churches if the pastor is responsible for more than one church. Many years ago, the Lord asked me to go to a particular church service. It was not my local church. I went. I knew the Lord wanted to teach me something. During the worship service, there was the washing of the feet ceremony. The Lord asked me to pay close attention. The pastor was washing his leadership team's feet. He was so gentle, and he performed it with such love. He truly had a servant's heart. I was in awe. There was just something about that man of God's heart. He was full of the Father's love. A few months later, I had a dream about this same man. In the dream, he had his hands up in worship and surrendering posture, and he told the Lord, "I have done everything you asked me to do." I woke up and pondered on the dream. I knew the man was ready to go home. Within six months, he was gone to be with his Lord and Savior. The Lord taught me that day that the pastor is to serve His people and not to be served himself or herself. This man of God was a servant, and his heart was very transparent. He was God's chosen vessel for that group of people, and he had served them well.

The Philadelphia Church, described in the book of Revelation, is a perfect example of a good church. The name *Philadelphia* means "brotherly love," and that is a good indication of what kind of people constituted this church; and to have a good church, there has to be a great leader who obeys God and seeks God's counseling, not only for himself or herself, but also God's people. S/he is an intercessor, who is constantly in prayer, seeking the will of God with every step and every decision. In Jesus' address to the Philadelphia Church, He reveals Himself as holy and true- the Alpha and Omega, the beginning and the ending, which is, and which was, and which to come, the Almighty. He is the one who has the key of David, and He opens doors that no one can shut and shuts doors that no one can open. He goes on to tell them that He had set an open door for them that no one could shut. That door is the door to evangelism. However, we know that there are always adversaries when we evangelize. The enemy conjures up many trials and temptations. He is the master manipulator and the author of confusion. He sets traps to bind and imprison God's people. He is good at defaming the believer's character, and he doesn't have a problem stirring pots to upset the peace. He sets obstacles in believers' midst that we must remove, and roadblocks that we must jump or climb over. Yes, if allowed, Satan can exhaust one out. Therefore, they had little strength; however, they were determined to finish the race. Thus, they did not deny Jesus' name, nor did they deny the Word of God, and continuing with the truth as they had in the past, Jesus would reward them by keeping them from trying temptation, which would come upon the earth. Not only that, but He would also make members of the synagogue of Satan, who were pretending to be Jews but were not Jews, to come and worship at their feet, and Jesus would also let the false Jews know that He loved them- the Philadelphia Church. In the end, they were to hold fast to their crown, that is the crown of life, life eternal; not allow anyone to take it from them, and those who overcame would make a pillar in the temple of God, and He would write upon them the name of His God and the name of the city of His God, and they would be given a new name. Isn't this what we all want? This is the "Well done my good and faithful servant," that all believers want to hear when we stand before the Father because God's chosen always puts God's people before his or her own needs. After all, that is what great leaders do-serve!

"Ye have not chosen me, but I have chosen you, and ordained you, that ye should go and bring forth fruit, and that your fruit should remain: that whatsoever ye shall ask of the Father in my name, he may give it you" (John 15:16 KJV). We know that God is the one who has chosen, called, equipped, and anointed us. However, before we discuss the true mantle, let's look at some coverings because while on earth, you need a pastoral covering, and not all pastors are like the one I described. Therefore, you must be careful who you align yourself with and have as your covering because they have charge over your soul. A friend of mine, and we will call her Abençoada, she aligned herself with someone she thought was a friend, who later became her pastoral covering. Little did she know that this person, and we shall call her Ciumenta, would act in Abençoada's life, even as King Saul did with King David. She could not handle where the Lord was leading Abençoada; henceforth, she became very vicious. Abençoada got sick, and for months, she suffered from a mysterious disease. You know what some call them? "Dis ease". The doctors could not find what was wrong with her. She suffered and suffered. She fasted and prayed, and she prayed continuously, knowing that her Lord Jesus is her healer. Her family members knew what she was going through, and periodically they would ask her how she was feeling. She never lost her faith in the Word of God, nor did she lose her faith in her healer and deliverer, Jesus Christ, and she believed for her healing.

She would tell them, "It is only a matter of time before Jesus heals me. No matter what my situation is, He is still the healer." In the meantime, she kept asking the Lord why she wasn't healed.

One evening during Bible study, a friend of hers discerned her pain and discomfort, and she got very angry at the devil and said, "OH, NO! This is it, we are going to get rid of this today." She and the other sister in the Lord started praying with Abençoada for her healing and deliverance. During those months, Abençoada had not stopped any of her routine and non-routine activities. She kept obeying the Lord, and she remained faithful to her Lord no matter how bad she felt. The sister knew that, and she recognized that her suffering was demonic. Now, Abençoada knew that as well, but she could only be delivered under the anointing of the Holy Spirit. That evening was it. They prayed with her until she was delivered. The demons were not in her because she is a Holy Spirit-filled Christian, and the Holy Spirit does not share His house with demons. In the meantime, her so-called covering attacked her in so many ways and by surprise. She did not know what hit her. She was puzzled because nothing out of line had happened between them. Her "pastor" had accused her of being racist due to her association with a reputable Christian organization that ministered to minority male students, helping them close the education gap. The education gap for minority boys is no secret in the United States, with studies showing that prisons estimate their future bed numbers by the number of students who cannot read by third grade, and this organization is doing what we all should have been doing to close the education achievement gap. Most do not know what equity means. Abençoada tried to explain to her "friend" the need for organizations as such, but to no avail. She had already made up her mind that they were an evil organization and that her church would have no part in it, and if she wanted to continue her association with the church, she had to cut all ties with that Christian organization. Abençoada refused the pastor's demands, and that set the pastor off and she went after her with a vengeance. She did everything in her power to destroy her character and ministry. She even wrote Abençoada a letter forbidding her all sorts of ministry. The way the letter read, Abençoada couldn't even minister to her children. She tried to silence her for good unless she agreed to her demands. Abençoada refused and the pastor went berserk. She contacted many of Abençoada's brothers and sisters in Christ. She told them that Abençoada was full of demons, and they should have nothing to do with her and her ministry. What Abençoada did not know is that she had been the one who was the cause of her sickness. She had been sending demons to harass her. Now, I know you are wondering how she knew. At first, she did not know because she had never suspected that her pastor would have done her wrong; especially that way, but after she began to contact all the ministers in their circle, she realized that she had been a friend to this woman, but the woman had never been a friend to her. It was during the prayer that the Holy Spirit revealed to her the source of the sickness. The words that came out of her mouth in prayer were inspired by the Holy Spirit, and she did pay attention to what He was saying through her and those praying for her deliverance. Yes, she was right. Abençoada was dealing with evil spirits. The ones she had been sending her way. You see, many times we have warning signs, but we either make excuses or we deny them. Throughout their friendship, there had been many warnings, but Abençoada had disregarded them to her demise. She always said that her "friend" was having a bad day or she was being harassed by the enemy and just prayed for her, but she should have run when her so-called friend told her that their former pastor had asked Abençoada to preach while he was on a pastors' retreat only to make her jealous, or when she discouraged her from studying and getting her college education, or when she tried to destroy her daughter's marriage before it even started. Yes, the warning sign was there, but she did not want to believe the worst of this "sister." After all, she was a true friend to her, and she did love her as Christ has commanded us to do. However, it was time for her to accept what had happened and was happening.

Later, as she meditated on her past situation, she realized that her "covering" had not prayed for her healing, even when she audibly and face-to-face had asked her to pray for her. There was a time that she told her that she did not care anything about the sickness she had. When Abençoada told her about her refusal to pray for her, she told her that she did not remember, but she did not deny it, either.

You are wondering if she prayed for her that day; no, she still did not do it. Abençoada thought about an incident where she was under demonic attack after returning home from a mission's trip abroad where her friend, then, did not pray for her either, and later told her that she did not pray for her because she perceived that she would not have received from her. As Abençoada puts it, "God used a donkey, He can use anybody." She said to her, "I was so hurting at that moment I would have received prayer from a dog if God had sent it." During that time, Abençoada felt like she was having a heart attack, and she never gave the testimony concerning her mission's trip abroad because she could not. The demonic attack was real, and she wasn't in a place conducive to that type of praise report. It took a brother in the church to leave his seat and cross the corridor to pray for her relief from the demonic attack. The sister who went with Abençoada was attacked as well. She was supernaturally hit in the mouth and couldn't even pray for Abençoada. It was clear that she had to break ties between her and this "pastor" who had also rescinded her ordination of Abençoada and had demanded the ordination certificate and other documents be returned to her immediately. Little did this pastor know, the Lord had instructed Abençoada to be ordained by another Christian organization. Although, Abençoada at the time did not know why she had followed the prompting of the Holy Spirit. After all was over, she understood why the Holy Spirit had moved her in that direction. Abençoada knows that nothing surprises God, because He is all-knowing.

During that Holy Spirit-anointed prayer, a severing took place. The Lord had Abençoada cut the cords and break the connection between her and the "pastor." Soul ties had to be cut and never to be put together again. A few days before all of these happened, Abençoada had been studying the seven churches of the book of Revelation. In her studies, she understood that there are some things in the local churches and the universal Church that are not of God. Will she accuse this pastor of having evil spirits? I don't know. All she knows is that the Jezebel spirit was in operation. No one has the right to strip a Christian of his or her Christian duties, especially those who are called into the ministry of Jesus Christ and have not done anything unscriptural. I told her not to worry because God causes the stumbling blocks set before us by our enemies to become stepping stones to higher heights and greater dimensions in Him, and that she would come through this victoriously because of her love, faith, and commitment to her Lord and Savior, Jesus Christ. Not too long after that, she reported that one of the ministries that the "pastor" had contacted to do her harm had backfired because the pastor and his wife had called and asked her to fast and pray and seek to see if the Lord would have her come and work with them full-time in their ministry, and they offered to set her up with her local church, should the Lord so led.

They told her that the work was great, and they needed her in ministry with them. What the enemy intended for evil, God had turned for her good.

Another friend of mine, and we will call her Rosa, attended a church for five years. She obeyed the leading of the Lord. At first, during the honeymoon period, things went well. Then, it seemed that all went down the hill. However, she stayed, and she prayed and prayed for the Lord to move in her church; she loved those people. She was determined to fight the spiritual battle. But sometimes it is best to move and not force things, especially when she perceived that she was fighting alone. She knew her season there was over, but she would not make a move without the leading of the Holy Spirit. She just prayed about her situation. It came time to make the move, and she went to her pastor and she asked him to release her from the church membership. They met in his office, and it seemed like the conversation was going well until he could not convince her to stay, and not that he tried hard either. All he could say was, "Did the Lord tell you to leave?" Repeatedly, she told him, 'Yes, Pastor.' His reasons for her staying was not good, and truth be known, it was just a monetary decision on his part. She could not stay. He believed that the Lord had not spoken, but he was incorrect. She had heard from the Lord. She remembers asking him several times to pray with her and for her, but he never responded. She realized he was not going to do it, so she said goodnight and goodbye, but not before she told him that he had her information, and if he ever needed her, he knew how to get in touch with her. She was an ordained pastor, but this denomination did not recognize female pastors. Not too long after she left the church, she became ill with something that seemed to be natural. But before I tell you about it, let me share something the Lord had showed her many years before attending this church.

One day, there was a visiting minister from out-of-state. She had been ministering at another church in the morning, and she was ministering at the church where Rosa was in the afternoon. She arrived a little late because the morning service had gone a bit longer than expected. So, the afternoon service was already in progress when she arrived. They had been worshiping for quite some time. She felt an evil presence come in, and she opened her eyes and looked around. Just then, the minister walked to the pulpit. She saw an evil spirit suspended in the air at her mid-back, following her. She asked the Lord what was that all about and what did He want her to do about the vision. She just prayed and waited on the Lord. She knew He wanted to teach her something. Next, He told her, "My people are looking for the anointing in others and want to be like them, but they do not get their anointing, what they get is the price they paid, and demons." She was flabbergasted with her mouth wide-opened. She said, "Wow, Lord." Later, after the minister had preached, she made an altar call, and Rosa said to herself, "I am not going up there. I'm good." Later, she observed a sister in Christ go up for prayer, and she came back to her seat worse off. Just then, she saw the demon. It looked like it was coming her way. Instantly, she moved as to move out of its way. Her oldest daughter was seated to her right on a seat next to her, and she moved. She said to her, "Did you see it?" She said, "No, but I've learned that when you move, I move." No sooner this happened, the sister crossed the aisle and came to Rosa for prayer with the demon following behind her. You see, demons move quickly. This one had been cast out and it was trying to find a new home. Rosa did pray for her sister in Christ. Then, immediately after, she cast the demon out, she could hear cars screeching on the street. She then commanded it to leave and go to the place the Lord had prepared for it, and not to do any harm to anyone. It left. I shared Rosa's account to let you know that you do not want anyone's mantle, but your own, given to you by God the Father, through His Son, Jesus the Christ. Now, let's go back to the situation with the pastor.

Before I tell you about it, I must fill you in with some details. After Rosa left the church, by the grace of God, she was promoted and validated in various areas of her life. However, she got ill with something that seemed to be normal. She fasted and prayed against it for a long time. She kept asking the Lord for a word. She knew one word from the Holy Spirit, and she would be healed instantly. She searched her heart to make sure she had nothing against anyone. She forgave everyone who had hurt her or even said things that they had no right to say to her. She asked God to forgive her part in it, and she forgave them and put them in God's hands, so they, too, could be delivered. In the meantime, she still made many visits to the doctors' office. She had several intrusive tests done. One test showed a whole lot of wrong, but the specialist could not tell all it was. She said to the Lord, "Your Word declares that you show no respect for a person." She said to Him, "You healed many just the last two weeks while I was ministering the Word of God." She saw it, and God had used her to deliver the message that brought the signs and wonders after the preaching of the Word. She further said, "Lord, you have a week to heal me before I go back to this next test." She went and did the test, and nothing was found. Everything was fine, praise the Lord. The rest of the tests were done with nothing showing. They were just trying to find the cause of the illness. Her quality of life was deteriorating and fast. She started aging due to sleep deprivation. The enemy attacked her at her job, and she wondered if she would even have a job at the end of the year; she wondered if she should retire early, quit and look for another job, or just keep on fighting for her position. The Lord led her to fight. Not just for her, but for those who would come after her. Her cause, you ask, justice. All these things were happening while she was asking the Lord to show her the cause of the illness. It wasn't until one morning, as she was talking to a sister in Christ, that she said something that triggered her thinking about a sister in the Lord who had attended the same church as she. The sister suffered from many diseases. Many times, she had said to her, "Take this sickness from me," and she would extend her hand to give it to Rosa." Each time, Rosa would say to her, "Jesus took that from you, put it on the Cross." This is one of the same things that Rosa had suffered for that long period. Every time she asked the Lord how she should pray, He would take her to a conversation the lady had with her husband concerning the side effects of her illness in front of Rosa. Rosa forgave her, she prayed for her. She released her to the Lord, and nothing. What Rosa did not understand is that both the lady and her husband had something to do with her health problem. Granted, it was the enemy using them because we are spiritual beings, and everything that happens to us begins in the spiritual realm. Her friend and sister in Christ said the "trigger word," and it caused her to go back and to see that she had been held in spiritual bondage. She was a slave to the spirit that was operating in her situation. She asked the Lord what kind of spirit was she dealing with that had such strong hold over her life. You see, she had given this person too much power over her life. She had looked at the person as her spiritual leader. She had even said that this person had lost the best daughter that he could ever have in her if only he had recognized the gift of God to him. Well, he was not worthy of her devotion, and it was wrong of her to put him in that place. In thinking that he was for her, she gave him too much honor; honor that belongs to the Father. She did not worship him, she wants you to understand this, but she did respect him in places that respect should not have been given. One should only follow and honor people in the areas that they are following and honoring Christ, the Lord. So, when it was time for her to move on, he did not release her. She realized that her illness was connected to both husband and wife. She needed to forgive them both, cut the spiritual umbilical cord, and move on with her Lord and Savior, Jesus Christ. I am here to report that she is free, and Jesus gets all the glory for her deliverance and her healing. Make sure you are connected to Christ first, and then others who are connected to Christ. You do not need, nor should you want the covering of those who are not aligned with God.

Another sister in Christ, not too long ago, shared with me that her pastor, before she went on to be with the Lord, prayed her mantle over her. Now, this would have been a nice gesture if we were living in the Old Testament; however, we are the New Testament Church, living in the New Testament purchased by the blood sacrifice and Resurrection of God's Son. Another interesting thing that happened with this transfer of mantle is that she received the mantle, but not this pastor's church, nor her ministries. Those went to another. What was the purpose of her mantle if she was not receiving her anointing and responsibilities? Isn't that what a mantle is? What was passed down were not the responsibilities and benefits of the mantle, rather the curses on that person's life, sickness, and disease. They were the headaches and pain. Nevertheless, I have ministered to her and prayed with her concerning this mantle. When I asked the Holy Spirit what spirits Rosa and this sister were dealing with, He told me the anti-Christ spirit. I said, 'well that is Satan himself." Rosa, and the other sister and I prayed against the antichrist spirit. We demolished his altar and broke it down to pieces, and then, we burned it to crisp and scattered the ashes, so it can never be put together against them and me ever again. *"Then did I beat them as small as the dust of the earth, I did stamp them as the mire of the street, and did spread them abroad" (I Sam. 22:43 KJV).* Anything that does not line up with the Word of God is satanic. Satan's altar placed on high places and attempting to take the throne of God in our hearts and lives must be destroyed. They rededicated their hearts and lives as I did, as well to the Lord Jesus. The deliverance prayer, which we had to say, went as follows: "Father, forgive me for my part in this. I chose to forgive myself, Lord. I reject and rebuke the antichrist spirit in my life. I tear down the altar of the enemy, and I cleanse my heart with the blood of Jesus. I clean up every cobweb in my heart with the hyssop (just then, I could see a stick the size of my arm with a cloth on the end of it with the blood of Jesus). I apply the blood to my heart, and I take it back and give it to you. Take my whole heart, Father, and take your place on the throne of my heart. Father, in the name of Jesus, purify it, cleanse it, and make it righteous, for you are righteous. Father, I need your blood transfusion. I ask that your blood, Jesus, flows through my veins, my arteries throughout my body, and purifies me from head to toes, inside and out. Thank you, Father, that I am made whole." Then, we read Luke 22:17-20, and received Communion. After, we sealed our Communion prayer with the anointing of the Holy Spirit and with the blood of Jesus, and by reading I Corinthians 11:24-25. Satan has a counterfeit for everything God has created. He tries to give us counterfeit coverings and mantles, but we must know the Word of God, refuse and reject his "giftings." He is a liar and the father of lies. He came to steal, kill, and destroy. But thank God for Jesus, our shepherd, who came to give us life more abundantly. *"The thief cometh not, but for to steal, and to kill, and to destroy: I am come that they might have life and that they might have it more abundantly" (John 10:10 KJV).*

Brothers and sisters, don't allow false coverings in your life. Be prudent. In the book of II Kings chapter 1, we see some coverings that were deadly as well as one that was wise. Ahaziah, king of Samaria, in his bed of affliction, inquired of the god Beelzebub, the god of Ekron, to see if he would recover from his disease, instead of enquiring from the God of gods, the God of Israel. Now, we know that our God is a jealous God. The king's action was not pleasing in God's sight, and he eventually dies according to the prophetic word sent to him from Elijah. However, not before others under his leadership died. After being rebuked by the prophet Elijah, who had sent him a message asking if there was not a God in Israel that he had inquired of the false god, the king sent a captain of fifty with his fifty men to bring Elijah down to him. Elijah calls fire from heaven, and the captain and his fifty men died. Then, the king sent a second captain of fifty with his fifty, and they had the same fate as the first set. The king sent yet a third captain of fifty with his fifty men. However, this third captain had a different approach to Elijah. He began by recognizing that Elijah was, in fact, a man of God, and he asked Elijah to spare his life and that of his men. The Angel of the Lord intervened and told Elijah to go down with him, assuring Elijah that the captain and his fifty men would not harm him. What was the difference? The fifty men's lives were saved because their covering, the captain, was wise in recognizing who Elijah was and honoring him with his speech and with his deed. So, you see, just as the wrong covering can get you killed, the right covering can save your life.

Having said all these, a covering is important. We must be accountable to someone, but please choose your covering carefully. You never want a lid or thumbs crushing down on you. In Jesus, there is freedom and liberty. No one has the right to control you. The Apostle Paul said to follow him as he followed Christ. *"Be ye followers of me, even as I also am of Christ"* (I Cor. 11:1 KJV). You are responsible for your salvation and your walk with Christ. You will stand before the Father and give an account for all you have done. It is not the pastor, it is you, and you alone who will stand before the Lord and give an account for what you have done with His Son's life given for you. Do not be suspicious of all you encounter, but please use discernment and make sure you follow those who are following Christ. If they are not, please watch over your soul. If you are currently under such ungodly leadership, break it! You must do it in a godly way, but do it for your soul's sake. Watch the leaders, study them before you commit to their input in your life. It can mean life or death. The "pastor" tried to kill Abençoada like Saul tried to kill David-the man after God's own heart; and just like Saul could not kill David, she couldn't either, but she did make Abençoada suffer for a while. The Bible says to know those who labor among you. *"And we beseech you, brethren, to know them which labour among you, and are over you in the Lord, and admonish you; And to esteem them very highly in love for their work's sake. And be at peace among yourselves" (I Thes. 5:12-13 KJV).* You must fast and pray and seek the Lord's discernment and wisdom before aligning yourself with anyone in this world; especially in ministry because of the agreements we confess righteous or unrighteous. Let's look at the agreement of two or three together. Often, when Christians are together, we quote the Scripture about Jesus being present when two or three are together in His name. We know, but how in-depth is our understanding of His presence? *"For where two or three are gathered together in my name, there am I in the midst of them" (Matthew 18:20 KJV).* We say that He never leaves us nor forsakes us, but how are we using this Scripture? Do we quote it but lack in understanding of its power? *"Let your conversation be without covetousness; and be content with such things as ye have: for he hath said, I will never leave thee, nor forsake thee" (Heb. 13:5 KJV).* Have we given these Scriptures the time and attention that they deserve, or are we just repeating what we heard others say? Pause and think. Jesus is, in fact, present as His Word declares, then, we must be elated in His presence.

One way I have utilized this Scripture is when I travel abroad where most do not know me. Some would take the opportunity to do whatever comes to their carnal minds and hearts. However, understanding that Jesus never leaves nor forsakes us gives me the confidence that I need to go everywhere He sends me, and my heart's behavior is constant because it is based on His presence and not fleshly desires. I know that He is with me even to the uttermost parts of the world. *"And Jesus came and spake unto them, saying, All power is given unto me in heaven and in earth. Go ye therefore, and teach all nations, baptizing them in the name of the Father, and of the Son, and of the Holy Ghost: Teaching them to observe all things whatsoever I have commanded you: and, lo, I am with you always, even unto the end of the world. Amen"* (Mat. 28:18-20 KJV). When you think of Jesus' presence, it is for all things according to His will, and we know that it is His will to keep us safe and to use us to bring salvation, healing, and deliverance to those we encounter. Meditate on the presence of the Lord right now. He is present, and He sees and hears all the concerns of your heart. He is present, but are you aware of His presence? I am reminded of a lesson the Holy Spirit taught me recently. I had catered a dinner function for a family member. I volunteered my services, but he paid for the food. He told me that he had transferred the dollar amount to my Apple account. I assumed the amount was going to show up on my bank account. Well, that is not how it works. The money was there for three weeks before I could access it. All I had to do was go to my Apple account and press a button to release it to my bank account. However, I had forgotten that I had to release it before it could go to my bank account. This may sound silly but stay with me there is a lesson. Jesus made provision for all our needs, and it is just sitting there in the bank of heaven. However, sometimes we do not know how to release our blessings. Therefore, they just sit there while we are in need. Just a word can release our provision, but we are at a loss for words, either by lack of knowledge or simply lack understanding how to operate in the treasures of heaven. Then, we want to beg God or blame Him for our inability to tap into heaven's resources. Let's listen attentively to the Spirit of the Living God, our great and mighty Father, and allow Him to teach us how to release our blessings. He is the teacher. In learning from the Holy Spirit, sometimes we must come boldly to the Throne of Grace. My brother-in-law was busy when I called him, but for some reason, he picked up my call. He then wanted to dismiss me, but I would not let him go until he instructed me on how to release the money from the Apple account to my bank account. Sometimes, we must be persistent with the Holy Spirit. Jacob wrestled with God and he would not let Him leave until He blessed him. *"And he arose that night and took his two wives, his two female servants, and his eleven sons, and crossed over the ford of Jabbok. He took them, sent them over the brook, and sent over what he had. Then Jacob was left alone; and a Man wrestled with him until the breaking of day. Now when He saw that He did not prevail against him, He touched the socket of his hip; and the socket of Jacob's hip was out of joint as He wrestled with him. And He said, "'Let Me go, for the day breaks.' But he said 'I will not let You go unless You bless me!' So, He said to him, 'What is your name?' He said, 'Jacob' And He said, 'Your name shall no longer be called Jacob, but Israel; for you have struggled with God and with men and have prevailed.' Then Jacob asked, saying, 'Tell me Your name, I pray.' And He said, 'Why is it that you ask about My name?' And He blessed him there. So Jacob called the name of the place Peniel: 'For I have seen God face to face, and my life is preserved.' Just as he crossed over Penuel the sun rose on him, and he limped on his hip"* (Gen. 32:22-31 KJV). Other times, we must listen attentively to the small still voice of the Holy Spirit if we want to learn and prosper in the Word. We must not take the Word of God out of context nor for granted. That is something that many do, due to lack of understanding to use the Word without the wisdom that comes with understanding the Word. I have heard many preachers use the following Scripture as a benediction; however, that is not the use of it as you will see: *"And Laban said to Jacob, Behold this heap, and behold this pillar, which I have cast betwixt me and thee: This heap be witness, and this pillar be witness, that I will not pass over this heap to thee, and that thou shalt not pass over this heap and this pillar unto me, for harm" (Gen. 31:51-52 KJV)*. However, it is used in the Bible as a prayer between Jacob and Laban as they part from each other to never come together again on the face of the earth and should either one break the prayer, they bring a curse on themselves. Yet, we have heard many use it as a benediction. Why is this? Many use it due to traditions and others out of lack of understanding and wisdom. The knowledge of the Scripture is there, but it is not coupled with understanding and wisdom. It is so important for us to allow the Holy Spirit to teach us as we read and meditate on the Word of God. The next time someone sent me money through the Apple account, I was quick to say to the person what it was that I had to do to release it, and she told me right there and then. Now, do you think I have to ask a third time? I doubt it, but if so, I will ask quickly as I have learned to ask the Holy Spirit and apply His teachings to my daily life. *"Wisdom is the principal thing; therefore, get wisdom: and with all thy getting get understanding" (Prov. 4:7 KJV)*. You do not want to be misled, nor do you want to mislead. Align yourself with those who are living for Christ and follow them as they follow Him. We live at a time when many false beliefs have crept into the Church, so we must be wise. *"For there shall arise false Christs, and false prophets, and shall shew great signs and wonders; insomuch that, if it were possible, they shall deceive the very elect" (Matt.24:24 KJV)*.

Reflection
Coverings

1. Identify the elements of a true covering and those of a counterfeit covering.
2. How is the Church of Philadelphia described?
3. Where did Abençoada go wrong in her relationship with Ciumenta?
4. Identify the spirit operating in Ciumenta. Explain.
5. What is the difference between oppressed and possessed?
6. Explain. Know those who labor amongst you.
7. What are soul ties?
8. What spirit is the Jezebel spirit, and how does it operate in the local church?
9. Why shouldn't you covet someone else's anointing?
10. In what areas has God promoted and validated you recently?
11. What is your opinion on someone wanting you to carry their sickness and disease for them?
12. What is the purpose of the transference of mantles?
13. Was the mantle transference done according to the Word of God? Why? Why not? Explain.
14. Who is responsible for your salvation?
15. With whom should you align yourself within ministry? Why?
16. How do you release your blessings in prayer?
17. Why must we apply Scriptures according to the Word of God?
18. Have you ever exercised your faith in prayer like Jacob? Explain.
19. According to Matthew 24:24, who or what shall arise?

Chapter 18

Fear No Evil

" *F* *or God hath not given us the spirit of fear; but of power, and of love, and of a sound mind" (2 Tim. 1:7 KJV).*

What is fear? Fear is an evil spirit that makes people feel threatened and it gives them a sense of harm that can be physical, emotional, or psychological; it may be real or imagined. For the most part, it is a trick of the enemy to paralyze you and cause you to live out of the will of God. It is not of God because God has given us the spirit of power, love, and sound mind. The areas that we fear are the areas that we are not trusting God; hence, we are not operating in His love. It is a sin against God. *"There is no fear in love; but perfect love casteth out fear; because fear hath torment. He that feareth is not made perfect in love" (I John 4:18 KJV).* I remember, as a baby Christian, I suffered from the spirit of fear. One day, it paralyzed me. I got up to go to the bathroom, just then it hit. I could not move. I needed to use the restroom or else. I was able to grab my Bible, and I turned to the two foundations and began to meditate on the solid foundation, Jesus Christ. I walked to the bathroom, reading the Bible out loud, and I held on to it the entire bathroom visit. I did not know what to do. It was fierce. Later during the week, I came across a very small book that addressed the spirit of fear. From that little book, I learned that fear was a sin against God, and since I did not want to sin against my Heavenly Father, I prayed and asked God to set me free from that evil spirit, and He did. Praise the Lord! I have been free since that day. Over the years, because I travel a lot, my students have asked me if I am not afraid of anything. My answer, "No!" He who the Son makes free is free indeed. *"If the Son therefore shall make you free, you shall be free indeed" (John 8:36 KJV).* Evil spirits are real, and they have powers.

Although Satan has powers, his powers are limited. He can only do what he is allowed; and according to the Bible, we are to bruise his head because Jesus did that already on the Cross, and we benefit from Jesus' sacrifice. *"And I will put enmity between thee and the woman, and between thy seed and her seed; it shall bruise thy head, and thou shalt bruise his heel" (Gen. 3:15 KJV).*

Satan has been put under our feet because of Jesus' power over him, and that power works in us and through us. *"And the God of peace shall bruise Satan under your feet shortly. The grace of our Lord Jesus Christ be with you. Amen" (Rom. 16:20 KJV).* Therefore, we do not fear his powers because as followers of Christ, Satan has no power over us. However, to exercise our authority over him and his demons, we must be obedient to God's Word and live with a pure heart and holy hands. We cannot live any old kind of way and think that we can fight and defeat him. Yes, Jesus took the keys of death and Hades, *"I am he that liveth, and was dead; and, behold, I am alive forevermore, Amen; and have the keys of hell and of death" (Rev.1:8 KJV),* but we have to do our part. We must know the Word of God, live right, that is according to the Word of God; then, we can fight the enemy and win because Jesus has won the victory, and we are victorious through Christ Jesus our Lord and Savior. *"But thanks be to God, which giveth us the victory through our Lord Jesus Christ" (I Cor. 15:57 KJV).*

Satan tries, but if you resist him, he will flee from you. *"Submit yourselves therefore to God. Resist the devil, and he will flee from you"* *(James 4:7 KJV)*. He is not omnipotent, nor is he omnipresent. Neither is he omniscient. He cannot be in all places at the same time. Only the Holy Spirit of God can. However, Satan has tried to portrait himself as omnipresent. What he has is an army with soldiers under him that he deputizes to torment those who do not know the Word of God. *"For we wrestle not against flesh and blood, but against principalities, against powers, against the rulers of the darkness of this world, against spiritual wickedness in high places"* *(Eph. 6:12 KJV)*. We must understand that we are at war with the enemy. The Bible says that the kingdom of heaven suffers violence, but the violent take it by force. *"And from the days of John the Baptist until now the kingdom of heaven suffers violence, and the violent take it by force"* *(Matt. 11:12 KJV)*. We must be sold out to who we believe in and let nothing, and no one prevent us from following Christ. Job did suffer violence, but he had a made-up mind to follow his God, and it did not matter what the enemy tried and did to him, he did not take his wife's ill advice to curse God and die. Satan could only do so much against him. Job was someone sold out to God, and God could say to Satan, "Have you considered my servant Job?" *"And the LORD said unto Satan, Hast thou considered my servant Job, that there is none like him in the earth, a perfect and an upright man, one that feareth God, and escheweth evil?"* *(Job 1:8 KJV)*

When we look at the life of Job, we see that God set some limitations on Satan to protect His people; so, Job was protected, and Satan could not cross those boundaries. Although Satan took everything precious from Job except his wife, He could not take his life because God told Satan that he could not kill him. *"Have You not made a hedge around him, around his household, and around all that he has on every side? You have blessed the work of his hands, and his possessions have increased in the land. But now, stretch out Your hand and touch all that he has, and he will surely curse You to Your face!" And the Lord said to Satan, "Behold, all that he has is in your power; only do not lay a hand on his person." So Satan went out from the presence of the Lord" (Job 1:10-12 KJV).* Jesus has given us His authority, so no weapon formed against us shall prosper, and everyone who comes against us in judgment we shall put them to shame. These people who come against you are sent by the devil himself because we do not fight against flesh and blood, but devils. Thanks to Jesus who has given unto us power over the enemy, and if we stay focused on God's Word, and submit to the Lord first, we will be like the Bible says, more than conquerors, as we use the authority in Christ over Satan. *"Submit yourselves therefore to God. Resist the devil, and he will flee from you" (Ja. 4:7 KJV).*

You must understand that as believers in Christ, you have authority over Satan and his demons. Our authority comes from Jesus, who has dominion over all, not just now, but throughout eternity. He has authority in heaven, on earth, and under the earth. He is omnipresent; therefore, His authority is everywhere in the universe. *"The eyes of your understanding being enlightened; that ye may know what is the hope of his calling, and what the riches of the glory of his inheritance in the saints, And what is the exceeding greatness of his power to us-ward who believe, according to the working of his mighty power, Which he wrought in Christ, when he raised him from the dead, and set him at his own right hand in the heavenly places, Far above all principality, and power, and might, and dominion, and every name that is named, not only in this world, but also in that which is to come: And hath put all things under his feet, and gave him to be the head over all things to the church, Which is his body, the fulness of him that filleth all in all" (Eph. 1:18-23 KJV).*

We inherited Jesus' power over the enemy. There is no question about it. The problem is that some of us do not know what was purchased for us on the Cross of Calvary due to lack of teaching and active studying and learning the Bible. Jesus is the head of the Church; so, if the body is aligned with the head, the body moves in tune with the head, Jesus Christ; thus, the body exercises the directives given by the head. Our spiritual eyes must be opened to see what God sees in us, what He has bestowed upon us through the death and resurrection of His only begotten Son, Jesus Christ. You do not have to fear the enemy. The enemy has to fear the One who has all power, and that is Jesus. Knowing that Jesus has you in the palm of His hand gives you the confidence to live the righteous and powerful life set before you by your God and Father. You do not have to fear the enemy, what you need is the discernment of spirits to be able to differentiate between good and evil, and to see the influences behind what you see and are experiencing. This gift of the Holy Spirit is vitally important in all Christians' lives if we are going to fight the enemy and win. The battle is spiritual, for we do not fight against flesh and blood. Therefore, we must know that Jesus has equipped us for the battle. We know that we win because Jesus has won the victory. He is our victor and He is the only potentate; the King of kings and the Lord of lords; hence, we do not fear our enemy, and he is our enemy because Jesus has no equals. We have to take back what the enemy robbed from us back in the Garden because Jesus has defeated him on our behalf. Jesus is the King! Satan is a pest. He is persistent, but you must be even more determined to take back what is rightfully yours. Imagine if Daniel had given up. He would not have received what he prayed for. It took the help of the archangel Michael to the archangel Gabriel for him to be able to go through the spiritual realm to deliver the message from God to Daniel. There is a spiritual war between good and evil. The Bible tells us that our warfare is not carnal, rather, it is spiritual. We do not fight against flesh and blood, as seen in Ephesians 6:10-20. Satan is a spirit; therefore, we cannot fight him with flesh because flesh agrees with Satan, and that is why it is dangerous to walk in the lust of the flesh because flesh fights against everything godly. That is why I tell my flesh to shut up often and to submit to the Holy Spirit. We must fight in the Spirit using our authority in Christ with all the weapons that Jesus has provided for us. It's a spiritual fight, and we must be suited up for it. Therefore, we must put on the armor of God.

Let's examine why the armor is vitally important in the spiritual battle that we are always engaged in. The Apostle Paul tells us to be strong in the Lord and the power of the Lord's might. Notwithstanding, we can only be strong in the Lord when we are in submission to the Captain of the Lord's Host, Jesus Christ. We are not fighting each other or flesh and blood. We are fighting invisible enemies who are seated in high places in the kingdom of darkness. Therefore, we must know and understand who our enemy is – Satan; we must not use only knowledge, but it is imperative that we couple our knowledge with understanding and wisdom in the fight for lives. Understand, that just because you do not see it, it does not mean that it is not going on. That is why it an invisible enemy and battle that is fought in the spiritual realm. Hence, we put on the armor, which consists of the belt of truth. Truth comes from God and it is a weapon against the father of lies, Satan, and all his host of soldiers or demons. Next, we put on the breastplate of righteousness, which protects our heart and keeps our heart pure and holy before the Father and all else. Following, we prepare our feet with the Gospel of peace, the Good News. Bringing peace and hope to all where ever we go. The shield of faith keeps all the fiery darts of the enemy from reaching us, especially our hearts. Additionally, we put on the helmet of salvation. The helmet protects our mind, for the mind is the battleground. Therefore, the battle begins in the mind, and if our mind is protected and steadfast on the Lord, the enemy cannot bring all the crazy things it tries to communicate to us. We must fight the enemy with the next weapon, which is the sword of the Spirit, the Word of God. Jesus fought Satan with the Word during His forty-day fast. We can follow Jesus' example and do the same by fighting the enemy with the Word of God. Lastly, we pray in the Spirit. Praying in the Spirit is another weapon that many Christians have not used as they ought to. Praying in tongues is powerful because the enemy does not know what you are saying to the Father, and he is defeated because he cannot comprehend nor interrupt your conversation with the Father.

Let's be real. Satan hates us. First, we are created in God's image, then, heaven is his past home –a place he can never return to because iniquity was found in him; thus, he was kicked out of heaven for all eternity. However, heaven is our future and eternal home. He cannot take out his anger at God, so he tries to take it out on us, God's children, but we know that he likes to make himself bigger than what he is. The prophet Isaiah tells us that one day we will look at him and marvel at the things he did to mankind. We will see him as the nothing he is. *"How art thou fallen from heaven, O Lucifer, son of the morning! how art thou cut down to the ground, which didst weaken the nations! For thou hast said in thine heart, I will ascend into heaven, I will exalt my throne above the stars of God: I will sit also upon the mount of the congregation, in the sides of the north: I will ascend above the heights of the clouds; I will be like the most High. Yet thou shalt be brought down to hell, to the sides of the pit. They that see thee shall narrowly look upon thee, and consider thee, saying, Is this the man that made the earth to tremble, that did shake kingdoms; That made the world as a wilderness, and destroyed the cities thereof; that opened not the house of his prisoners? All the kings of the nations, even all of them, lie in glory, every one in his own house" (Isa. 14:14-18 KJV).*

Satan was mad and he is still mad. Only someone mad would try to be God. He was created to serve and to worship God, but he decided that he was the one to be served and worshiped. It did not go well for him; therefore, he is here on earth causing havoc. Nevertheless, we must not be afraid of him. What can he do to us? We are sons of God, and in Jesus' name, we have authority over him and all his demons. He is a defeated foe. We cannot allow him to bring fear. Satan is a liar and the father of lies, even as Jesus said in John 10:10. Satan came, and he comes to us to steal, kill and destroy; however, Jesus came to give us abundant life. So, Satan must be exposed by the Word of God because it is vitally important for us to know and understand the authority given to us by the Father through our Lord and Savior Jesus Christ over Satan and his demons. We cannot move in fear. We must move in the gift of the size of a mustard seed faith because that is all we need to defeat him. Let me tell you a story, a true account, before moving on.

Satan can no longer continue to be the liar and father of lies that he is in our lives when we submit to God. Recently, I visited a family member who was going through a divorce. I had visited her home many times in the past, and the place was a pleasant place to visit, except this time it was different. I was greeted by a stench at the front door. I asked her what that awful smell was? At first, she said it was fish, which she had fried a week prior. I knew different. She did not smell it, but I did. It was repugnant and irritating. It seemed to be throughout the house at first; however, later I noticed it was only in certain areas. I prayed the first night, but nothing happened. We were invited to dinner at another family member's home the next day. On the way back from dinner, we both noticed some strange things had happened in her car. I asked her if anyone else had keys to her car. She assured me that only she had the keys and she knew where they were the entire time. No one else had used her keys. We discussed the strange things, as I prayed silently. We arrived at the home. The first thing out of her mouth was, "*The* stench still here?" I said, "Yes." She said, "I want you to pray for the house and ask God to cleanse it." First of all, she gave me authority over her home for prayer, so I did. I took authority in Jesus' name and prayed in the Holy Ghost. I walked around her house as the Spirit let me. She stayed in the house. After I was done praying for the house, she asked me to pray for her. She had been suffering from vertigo for months. Her doctor was going to send her to a neurologist for tests. She had started to believe the lie of cancer. I prayed and God healed her instantly. She became a believer. This happened because she permitted me to pray in and around her home and for her, and I knew my authority in Jesus. The stench left, and the rest of my visit was pleasant. Her husband, unbeknown to her, was involved with a woman, and they were exercising witchcraft, trying to take her out so they could have all her possessions and live "happily ever after." Discernment of spirits was vitally important in this situation. I discern by the Spirit of the Living God that this was no fish smell, rather, that of evil spirits. Sometimes, we go places thinking we are just visiting, but we need to be opened to the Holy Spirit. My visit had a dual purpose. Thank God for His Spirit. After, I taught her how to take authority over her home and not allow the enemy to come back and torment her and her guests. Of all places, her husband selected a woman living directly across from their home to have the affair, and he did leave her for the woman. She was devastated. I asked her to forgive both of them so she can have peace in her life- the peace that surpasses all understanding. She is a beautiful, intelligent, and caring woman, and she is victorious through Christ Jesus. Satan thought he had her, but he lost because through all the torment, she gave her life to Christ Jesus, and she was set free from the hands of the enemy, and that is what the authority over the enemy is all about-setting captives free! Let's continue expounding on the authority of Jesus in our lives through the eyes of the mantle of the Father's heart.

Reflection
Fear No Evil

1. Who has the keys of death and Hades?
2. According to James 4:7, how can you get rid of Satan?
3. Can Satan do whatever he wants with us?
4. Where does our authority and power over the enemy come from?
5. What kind of battle are we engaged in?
6. Name each piece of the armor of God and do explain their function.
7. Who is the Captain of the Host, and where is He when we are engaged in spiritual battle?
8. According to Revelation 12:11, how do we overcome the enemy?
9. Name some benefits of the blood of Jesus
10. Identify a few reasons as to why Satan hates us.
11. According to Isaiah 14:14-18, who is Lucifer?
12. How is Satan exposed as a liar and the father of lies?
13. Identify an illness that was spiritual and not physical. Expound on it.

Chapter 19

The Mantle of the Father's Heart

Y ou asked, what is a mantle? What is power and what is
authority?

I am glad you asked.

A mantle is a cloak or a covering, and prophets in the Old
Testament were known for wearing them as a sign of their calling,
power, authority, and responsibilities as God's spokesmen. *"And
it was so, when Elijah heard it, that he wrapped his face in his
mantle, and went out, and stood in the entering in of the cave. And,
behold, there came a voice unto him, and said, 'What doest thou
here, Elijah?'" (I King 19:13 KJV) "And as Samuel turned about
to go away, he laid hold upon the skirt of his mantle, and it rent" (I
Sam.15:27 KJV). "He took up also the mantle of Elijah that fell
from him, and went back, and stood by the bank of Jordan; And he
took the mantle of Elijah that fell from him, and smote the waters,
and said, 'Where is the Lord God of Elijah?' and when he also had
smitten the waters, they parted hither and thither; and Elisha went
over. And when the sons of the prophets which were to view at Jericho
saw him, they said, 'The spirit of Elijah doth rest on Elisha.' And they
came to meet him, and bowed themselves to the ground before him"
(II Kgs. 2:13-15 KJV).*

There are godly and ungodly powers in the earth; therefore,
you must understand what power you are under because power

is the capacity or ability to direct or influence others' behavior or course of life's events. Consequently, the only power you want to be under is that of the Holy Spirit and those who are led by the Spirit of God. *"For as many as are led by the Spirit of God, they are the sons of God" (Rom. 8:14 KJV).*

People who have authority over you have the right to give you orders, make decisions for you, and enforce your obedience to what they tell you to do. Therefore, you must be very careful who you trust your soul to as you already saw what happens at times when you align yourself with the carnal or the false. The mantle of Jesus comes with the power and the authority of Christ. Not only does Jesus have the authority over all the earth, but He also has the power to enforce and accomplish whatever He wants. Think of a police officer, he does not have the power to physically stop your car on the road, but as soon as s/he puts that siren on, you better pull over and stop. That is authority. *"And the rain fell, and the floods came, and the winds blew and slammed against that house; and yet it did not fall, for it had been founded on the rock. Everyone who hears these words of Mine and does not act on them will be like a foolish man who built his house on the sand." "The rain fell, and the floods came, and the winds blew and slammed against that house; and it fell—and great was its fall. When Jesus had finished these words, the crowds were amazed at His teaching; for He was teaching them as one having authority, and not as their scribes"* (Matt. 7:25-29 KJV). Jesus spoke and taught with authority, and that authority He has given unto us, as you will see.

"For there is no respect of persons with God" (Rom. 2:11 KJV). *"Then Peter opened his mouth, and said, Of a truth I perceive that God is no respecter of persons: But in every nation, he that feareth him, and worketh righteousness, is accepted with him. The word which God sent unto the children of Israel, preaching peace by Jesus Christ: He is Lord of all" (Acts 10:34-36 KJV).* The Bible tells us,

sisters in Christ, that God is no respect of a person, so understand that the mantle is for you as well as men because if a woman can carry the child Christ Jesus (Matt. 1:16), you can certainly carry and deliver the Word of God, which is Jesus the Christ. *"In the beginning was the Word, and the Word was with God and the Word was God" (John 1:1 KJV).* Did not Deborah lead the army of Israel? (Judg. 4:10). Queen Esther was born for such a time to be an instrument God used to save His people Israel (Esther 5-10). Did not Mary Magdalene and the other Mary announce the resurrection of Jesus Christ? The Apostle Paul visited Aquila and Pricilla who were husband and wife (Acts 18:1-3, 18, 19, 26 KJV). Yes, these accounts are in the Book. If these do not convince you, read the books of Joel and Acts, where it states that in the last days God will pour out His Holy Spirit upon all flesh (Joel 2:28 and Acts 2:17). Who is He, the preacher and teacher in you, if not the Holy Spirit? Consider the fact that the Church and the Bride are addressed as feminine. Does that mean that men will not have their part in heaven with Jesus when He comes for His Bride? God forbid it! There, it is settled. The enemy is the one who has caused this confusion to divide God's people, so we are not as productive as we ought to be in the ministry of our Lord Jesus Christ. God is not looking at males nor is He looking at females. He is looking for a people who have pure hearts and clean hands, vessels yielded to His Holy Spirit. We cannot let the enemy, under the guise of religion nor traditions, keep us from the ministries God ordained for us.

The message that brought all this about was the message on the mantle of Christ Jesus. It came straight from the mouth of Jesus through the book of Matthew. Then Jesus came spake unto them saying, *"All power is given unto me in heaven and in earth. Go ye therefore, and teach all nations, baptizing them in the name of the Father and of the Son and of the Holy Ghost, teaching them to observe all things whatsoever I have commanded you: and, lo, I am with you always, even unto the end of the world. Amen" (Matt. 28:18 KJV).*

I was out-of-country ministering for a couple of weeks. I had already preached the Word multiple times, and it was always inspiring and inspirational. I would study, fast, and pray in preparation; however, the Lord would never give me the message until I picked up the microphone to preach. Sometimes, I had to pray just a little bit longer to hear the message for the house. Even then, it was as He was giving utterance. This day, He took me to Matthew 28:18. And He began to expound on the Scripture. The Holy Spirit spoke through me like never. He took every and any excuse that all attending men and women alike could have used to disobey the Lord. He left nothing unturned. At the end of the message, the entire church, except the pastor, received the Holy Spirit with the evidence of speaking in tongues. The pastor, a Holy Spirit-filled man of God, got a brand-new church that day. His entire congregation was filled, bringing a new season in their lives and the church. Before the message, the Holy Spirit had told the congregation that that day was the beginning of a new chapter for them. We just did not understand what He was saying until after the message. The Holy Spirit removed every and any excuses that the people may have had from previous erroneous lessons on the Holy Spirit and those of disobedience in doing what God had called them to do. He also expounded on the authority of Christ in them. The mantle was made plain and simple to comprehend. Even a child could have understood it. At least, to the degree He wanted us to understand it, or we could contain at that time.

I came home a few days later, and I have not been the same. The Father continued to teach me about the mantle of Jesus Christ, but before He addressed Jesus' mantle, He showed me several other coverings as it has been written in the Covering chapter.

The enemy wants you to be unproductive for the kingdom of God by keeping you ignorant of your mantle. This is what the Father wants for you and me. When He began to reveal the mantle, I was in awe and still am. There is so much power in the mantle of Jesus.

In the New Testament, we have the mantle of Jesus. In the Book of Matthew, you see that Jesus releases His mantle to us by saying that all authority had been given to Him in heaven and earth and there He commands or commissioned us to go to all the nations of the world and preach the Gospel. Jesus gave us His authority, so we can go out and minister. He further said that He would be there present with us. He said, *"And Jesus came and spake unto them, saying, All power is given unto me in heaven and in earth. Go ye therefore, and teach all nations, baptizing them in the name of the Father, and of the Son and of the Holy Ghost: Teaching them to observe all things whatsoever I have commanded you: and, lo, I am with you always even unto the end of the world. Amen"* (Matt. 28:18-20 KJV).

Jesus said that we did not choose Him, but He chose us. *"Ye have not chosen me, but I have chosen you, and ordained you, that ye should go and bring forth fruit, and that your fruit should remain: that whatsoever ye shall ask of the Father in my name, he may give it you"* (John 15:16 KJV). He goes on to say that we are to bring forth fruits, and fruits that remain, and that is souls. We must preach the gospel of Jesus Christ. And we can only do it boldly when we know the authority and the anointing of God through the mantle of Jesus. After I had ministered the Word on the authority of Jesus in our lives, I continued to talk with the Holy Spirit about this ministry power and authority Jesus has given us. I said to Jesus, "You did not call the legions of angels because you had to go to the Cross so I can call them." I said, "Your Word is true," and I said then, "I am calling a legion of angels to go before me, and minister in my workplace." A few days later, I prayed with a sister in Christ, and I released a legion of angels in her life, and within twenty minutes, she called me, all excited, to give her testimony. She had gone to a local store to do some shopping. While in the store, a Christian brother from out-of-state, whom she did not know, approached her and said to her, "Oh, my God! You are a minister of the Gospel, aren't you? I know you are because you have a legion of angels around you." The brother then proceeded to call his wife because he wanted her to see what he was seeing. I was excited as well because this was confirmation that Jesus' authority or mantle was working in my life. I had released a legion of angels, but the Holy Spirit wanted me to look at the amount for future dispatching. He sent me to the book of Matthew, chapter 26:53. I said, "Oh, my God!" Twelve and more legions of angels is what Jesus wants; perhaps, the sister only needed one legion, but in the future, the Lord wanted me to dispatch twelve or more angels. Don't get me wrong. Like most, I had read this Scripture many times, but followed the prompting of the Holy Spirit and dispatched only one legion, but there is a time and season for everything, and the Father wanted me to be ready. I did the math. 6,000 is a legion and 6,000 times twelve is 72,000 angels. I was in awe and said, "Well, that is just the minimum because Jesus said twelve or more." What is more? More has no limitations. The Shinto religion has 8 million demons, and I said "That is nothing to Jesus. We have at our disposal an unlimited number of angels to help in kingdom work." By now, you know that I always ask God for confirmation in everything He is teaching me, so He took me to 2 Kings chapter 6. There, we find out that Elisha asked the Lord to open the eyes of the young man, so he could see that those who were with them were more than those who were against them, and God did open the young man's eyes. At this point, I have three different Scriptures: Matthew 26:5, Matthew 28:18-20, and 2 Kings 6. I do this because by the witness of two or three a thing is established according to the Word of God. I do trust God, but in a multitude of counsel, I will not err, and what better council than His Word?

The authority of Jesus in our lives is not to be abused or misused. It is to be used for the building and the furthering of God's kingdom. The Power of the Mantle is in the faith to believe that what Jesus said and imparted to us is the absolute truth. There is no wavering. You must know that you know that you carry His mantle. Father God did not send His only begotten Son for naught. It behooves us to take it seriously. When you know in your knower that it is yours to carry, you will use it with fear; that is reverence and trembling. It is what some say a heavy mantle, but I say it is the only mantle. Counterfeit mantles are for the ignorant and the cowardly. Believers must be bold and courageous, reverencing God and fearing nothing. You do not fear the enemy because you have the Word of God, you have the Name above all names, Jesus, you have the blood of Jesus, you have the Father and the Holy Spirit of the Living God, you have the armor of God, and you have legions of angels, and all on your side as you work for the kingdom of your Heavenly Father. Yes, Satan tries to intimidate, and he tries to appear bigger than what he is, but don't you know Jesus defeated him already? Don't you know that Jesus and all He is and has are at your disposal? Yes, you got this! Go forth and do what God the Father has ordained for you to do. I know, I am. Pray, preach, and teach with authority, and watch the Holy Spirit perform miracles in Jesus' ministry through you. He loves you, and He loves His people. He is with those who are humble before Him. Know that He is behind His Word to perform it. He does it through you. Give Him all your praise and your worship, and you will go far in Him. And when you stand before Him, He will say, "Well done, my son!" "Well done, my daughter!"

The mantle is not free. Jesus went through unspeakable pain and suffering before and during the Cross. Imagine the beating He took that He was unrecognizable. How about the crown of thorns that was thrust upon His head? In 2002, I was in South Africa ministering with some brothers and sisters. We stayed in a house, and in the garden was a small acacia tree, nicknamed in Africa, the *Devil's Thorns*. It has long thorns of approximately 8-10 centimeters long, and they are sharper than knives. I touched one gently to see what it felt like while I was thinking about what Jesus must have gone through with the crown of thorns. I cannot begin to imagine nor describe the pain He must have felt as they forcefully shoved the crown of thorns on His head. How about the 39 lashes that the soldiers brutally gave Him, and as they struck Him, pieces of flesh were torn from His body, the mocking and the plucking of the bear, the spitting and the insults by the thief who was crucified side by side with Him? How about the rejection of His people and town? Do you think that God the Father who gave Him for us is pleased when we cheapen the Cross of His Son? No! Jesus took all that pain and suffering and the anguish of His soul, so He could present us with the authority and power He earned with His sweat, blood, and life. How can we do anything but believe and exercise the authority and power of Jesus? Not doing so is dishonorable to the Father and the Son. When I think of this, I am compelled to exercise the authority and power that is in the mantle of Jesus Christ. My belief is based on His sacrifice, and I would hate to waste Jesus' life in mine. I know the Father would not be pleased. He did give us His very best, so we must give back to Him our very best. I am grateful that the Holy Spirit has revealed this truth to me. It has increased my faith, and God's anointing in my life is greater. I know that I honor the Father when I exercise the authority and power in the mantle that He prepared for me in Jesus, and I love Him the more for it. The mantle of Jesus is my mantle. I have no desire for any other mantle; especially since I know that all others are counterfeit. I embrace the mantle of the Father's heart for me, and I am mandated to teach it, to preach it, and to use it in prayer. The mantle of Jesus is your mantle as well. Do you desire the truth? Do you want to move in tune with the Father, the Son, and the Holy Spirit? Do you want the glory Jesus gave to you?

"At that day ye shall know that I am in my Father, and ye in me, and I in you" (John 14:20 KJV). Jesus said that we would know that He and the Father are one and that we are in Him as He in us makes us one with Him and the Father. Furthermore, He said in His prayer for us that He gave us His glory, so we could become one with Him and the Father. *"And the glory which thou gavest me I have given them; that they may be one, even as we are one" (John 17:22 KJV).* He goes on to say that the glory is so we are perfect, and that the world may know that God sent Him, and that God loved us, and He loved Jesus. How amazing is this, and what is His glory?

The Apostle Paul said that all have sinned and come short of the glory of God; however, Jesus has come for the restoration of God's glory in our lives. *"For all have sinned and come short of the glory of God; being justified freely by his grace through the redemption that is in Christ Jesus: Whom God hath set forth to be a propitiation through faith in his blood, to declare his righteousness for the remission of sins that are past, through the forbearance of God; To declare, I say, at this time his righteousness: that he might be just, and the justifier of him which believeth in Jesus" (Rom. 3:23-26 KJV).* With sin, we are stripped naked from the glory of God because we can only show God's infinite beauty to others when we are in right standing with Him. I remember a time when God asked me to paint a picture of Him and to paint it well. This was a message about His glory. It was to show His infinite goodness, mercy, compassion, and beauty. People need to see and experience God's love through us, and that is how we show His glory to the world. Jesus is our example; He came and showed God's glory to the world through His ministry. He healed the sick, cleansed the lepers, raised the dead, cast out devils, opened deaf ears and blind eyes, and much more. He showed God's glory to mankind, and that is the reason He gave us His glory, so we can do the same.

Then, the mantle of the Father's heart is yours for believing, receiving, and using. It is the mantle for all who desire the truth. Understand that with the mantle of the Father's heart comes the title deed of earth. We are the rightful owners. Jesus took the ownership that Satan stole from us using Adam and Eve back in the Garden of Eden, and He has given it back to us through His authority and power in His mantle. We are to take back from Satan by force all that he has stolen from us. We are the heirs; the ones who inherit the kingdom of our God and Father through His Son, Jesus Christ's death. *"And if children, then heirs; heirs of God, and joint-heirs with Christ; if so be that we suffer with him, that we may be also glorified together" (Rom. 8:17 KJV).*

The Holy Spirit instructed me to receive Communion seven days straight. During this time, He taught me and continues to teach me about the power in the blood of Jesus. You see, the mantle is all about what the Blood purchased for us. He has shown me that as children of the Creator and created in His image and likeness, that he has given us creative power. He had me look at my hands and see what He has gifted me for His glory. I can also use the power in the spoken Word to call those things that aren't as if they were. Believe the Bible when it tells you that there is power in the spoken Word. *"Death and life are in the power of the tongue: and they that love it shall eat the fruit thereof" (Prov. 18:21 KJV).* He has shown me through Communion that in Luke 22:15-20 that there were two cups mentioned, which led me to research and learn more about the cups. In the Jewish Passover ceremonies, there were four cups of wine. Jesus begins with the third cup, according to Luke, and gives the fourth cup to His disciples to take and drink in remembrance of Him. Just then, I began to wonder what significance any number four has. I was in for a world of discoveries. But before I could do the study of the number four, I was stuck on I will not drink this cup until the kingdom of God has come. It wasn't until after Jesus' death and resurrection that the kingdom of God fully came. This is very significant because the mantle of Jesus is all about the kingdom of God being done on earth as is in Heaven. *"Thy kingdom come. Thy will be done in earth, as it is in heaven" (Matt. 6:10 KJV).*

The prayers are authoritative and with conviction. Heaven is perfect, and if we want certain things to happen here on earth, we must exercise the authority and power in the mantle of Christ Jesus. Jesus taught and spoke with authority. The only places that He could not do much were the places where they lacked faith and they were disrespectful to Him. He said that a prophet is without honor in his town. Don't waste your time in those places. Do as Jesus did; leave and go where you are received, and God is honored. Don't waste God's given time and Jesus' anointing in your life. Move in tune with His Holy Spirit. He will guide and lead you. Make sure you keep your heart pure and your hands clean at all times and ready for worship and service. The harvest is plentiful, but the laborers are few; therefore, don't waste your time trying to please those you will never be able to please. You must know and understand that they are not going where God has ordained for you to go and minister. This is serious business, and you cannot wait for those who do not understand the call of God in your life. The Father's business is focused on those who are dying and going to hell. You must snatch them, and there is an urgency to bring them from the kingdom of darkness into His kingdom of light. God loves His people. You must understand and recognize that some are not yours, and do not try to become something or someone to those God did not ordain you to be theirs. You must recognize your assignment and those you have been assigned to, and not allow the enemy's distractions.

Years ago, I spent a lot of time trying to convert a lady who was involved in witchcraft. That was a waste of my time. I spent unproductive time with her, and later, I understood that the enemy had sent her to distract me and take me off focus on what God wanted and needed me to do. I repented and moved on. She loved what she was doing, and she did not want to be delivered. Today, if you were to see her, you would not recognize her. Her sins have caught up with her, and she spends her time in the emergency room and the hospital, going from one surgery to another. I pray she gets set free soon. We all have been given a will to choose between good and evil. When we choose evil, that is the bread we bake and eat. Satan has nothing good to offer. He only makes promises he cannot, nor intend to keep. He cannot give good gifts; it's out of character for him to be good; besides, what he offers you is already yours through Jesus Christ. Don't be deceived. Stay connected to the seven Spirits of God and go forth in Jesus' name. *"John to the seven churches which are in Asia: Grace be unto you, and peace, from him which is, and which was, and which is to come; and from the seven Spirits which are before his throne" (Rev. 1:4 KJV).*

God is Light, and nothing is in darkness in Him because He can illuminate your path; therefore, you do not need to fear the stumbling blocks that the enemy set before you. Your Father gives you dreams and visions, and if He has to put you in a trance, He will, and He will allow you to hear audible conversations that will either keep you going in the right direction or reroute you; therefore, do not fret. Nothing escapes the Holy Spirit. He is seven Spirits, complete. *"And out of the throne proceeded lightnings and thunderings and voices: and there were seven lamps of fire burning before the throne, which are the seven Spirits of God" (Rev. 4:5 KJV).* Know that the Holy Spirit is all-knowing and all-seeing, and He sees everything. Just rely on Him, and He will lead you in the right path, always. *"And I beheld, and, lo, in the midst of the throne and of the four beasts, and in the midst of the elders, stood a Lamb as it had been slain, having seven horns and seven eyes, which are the seven Spirits of God sent forth into all the earth" (Rev. 6:5 KJV).*

When you operate in the mantle of the Father's heart, you have all that it contains at your disposal. It is the mantle of Jesus, and as you can see in Isaiah, all is there. The mantle is lacking in nothing. Hence, you lack in no area. Just obey the Father, and the Spirit of Jesus Christ will rest upon your life as well, and you will see as Jesus sees. You will not inspect the fruit in peoples' lives with your natural eyes nor ears. You will see what the Father sees and hears. *"And the spirit of the Lord shall rest upon him, the spirit of wisdom and understanding, the spirit of counsel and might, the spirit of knowledge and of the fear of the Lord; And shall make him of quick understanding in the fear of the Lord: and he shall not judge after the sight of his eyes, neither reprove after the hearing of his ears" (Isa. 11:23 KJV).* You are well equipped to go and please the Father. It's His heart. Recently, I had a vision where I saw the train of Jesus' mantle, and I could see that all who trust the Lord and placed themselves under the train of His mantle are covered and protected. The train was long and wide, and it ran far where I couldn't see its end. There is no end to God's protection over your life; so, live without fear and trust in God by allowing your faith in Christ to move you. Therefore, go ye! It's your mantle!

Reflection
The Mantle of the Father's Heart

1. What is a mantle?
2. What is the difference between power and authority?
3. Define godly and ungodly powers.
4. Who has spiritual authority over you, and how have they exercised their authority?
5. Does God discriminate? Support your answer with Scriptures.
6. How would you respond to the following statement: The mantle of the Father's heart is reserved for men only.
7. Unproductivity in the kingdom of God is due in part because of lack of knowledge. Explain your position concerning this statement.
8. Who is Jesus talking to when He says, "Go ye therefore..." in Matthew 28:18-20?
9. What is your takeaway on the prayer of legions of angels?
10. What is the purpose of the authority of Jesus given to us?
11. Who is to carry the mantle?
12. Who tries to appear bigger than he is, and why?
13. The mantle is not free. Explain.
14. Is the mantle of Jesus your mantle? Explain.
15. For what purpose did Jesus give us His glory?
16. The Apostle John said that if all the things Jesus did were written, the world would not be able to contain them. Explain.
17. What is the power of the tongue?
18. What is the Father's business focused on?
19. Does Satan intend to keep his promises? Why? Why not?
20. Name a few ways that God communicates with you?
21. Who sees everything, and why must you trust Him?
22. Name the seven Spirits of God.

Tailored Mantle

You have been chosen, called and ordained by God to carry the mantle of His heart. Why then would you desire someone else's mantle? It is unpretentious. The enemy places distraction in your path to cause you to miss God. But we are not ignorant of his devices. Let's take a look at King David's life. Saul wanted him to wear his armor to fight Goliath. King Saul, as Scriptures describe him, was a head taller than all the men around him, and David, at that time, was said to be a shepherd boy. Saul's armor was too big for David; even though David later would become king of Israel. King Saul's armor, or we can say mantle, was tailored for him and him alone. "And Saul said to David, Go, and the LORD be with you! So Saul clothed David with his armor, and he put a bronze helmet on his head; he also clothed him with a coat of mail. David fastened his sword to his armor and tried to walk, for he had not tested *them*. And David said to Saul, I cannot walk with these, for I have not tested *them*. So David took them off. Then he took his staff in his hand; and he chose for himself five smooth stones from the brook, and put them in a shepherd's bag, in a pouch which he had, and his sling was in his hand. And he drew near to the Philistine. So the Philistine came, and began drawing near to David, and the man who bore the shield *went* before him. And when the Philistine looked about and saw David, he disdained him; for he was *only* a youth, ruddy and good-looking. So the Philistine said to David, *Am* I a dog, that you come to me with sticks? And the Philistine cursed David by his gods. And the Philistine said to David, Come to me, and I will give your flesh to the birds of the air and the beasts of the field! Then David said to the Philistine, You come to me with a sword, with a spear, and with a javelin. But I come to you in the name of the LORD of hosts, the God of the armies of Israel, whom you have defied. This day the LORD will deliver you into my hand, and I will strike you and take your head from you. And this day I will give the carcasses of the camp of the Philistines to the birds of the air and the wild beasts of the earth, that all the earth may know that there is a God in Israel. Then all this assembly shall know that the LORD does not save with sword and spear; for the battle *is* the LORD's, and He will give you into our hands. So it was, when the Philistine arose and came and drew near to meet David, that David hurried and ran toward the army to meet the Philistine. Then David put his hand in his bag and took out a stone; and he slung *it* and struck the Philistine in his forehead, so that the stone sank into his forehead, and he fell on his face to the earth. So David prevailed over the Philistine with a sling and a stone, and struck the Philistine and killed him. But *there was* no sword in the hand of David. Therefore David ran and stood over the Philistine, took his sword and drew it out of its sheath and killed him, and cut off his head with it" (I Sam. 17:37-51 KJV). King Saul needed a full armor to engage in battle to fight the Philistines, and up to that point, he and the army of Israel had not defeated the enemy, but all David needed was his sling shot and five stones. David knew how to operate in his own anointing. King Saul's armor, mantle, and anointing were unfamiliar to him, and as he stated, he had not tried Saul's armor; however, he was an expert with his sling, and his anointing was in no way lacking. It worked. He killed Goliath with one stone, and if anyone else was up to the challenge, he had four more left and could take care of them as well. Furthermore, why would King David want to wear Saul's armor when he would become part of the lineage of Jesus Christ, and Saul and his bloodline had no part in it? Meditate on this, especially when you are looking at someone with covetous eyes concerning his or her anointing. The enemy highlights all the fine details of someone's mantle, making it look very attractive, to the point that you envision yourself dressed up in that particular mantle. But can you pay the price of its operation, or are you even called to pay the same price for the operating anointing in that person's life? No! Our walk with God is unique. Although the mantle of Jesus Christ is the same in power and authority, it is tailored according to our calling and walk and operation with the Father. The price we pay for the anointing is according to our calling. Just as you can't live my life, you cannot have my personalized mantle, I cannot live your life, therefore, I cannot carry your anointing or your tailored mantle.

Hopefully, the mantle that those around you carry are authentic. But imagine for a moment wanting a person's mantle who, unbeknown to you, has been operating under the control of the Jezebel spirit. How devasting will it be when you find out that you have been deceived and in need of deliverance from the counterfeit spirit. Another is that of people wanting a particular disciple's anointing. This is wrong on many levels, but I will dismantle the tactics of the enemy with a few examples.

The Apostle Peter is one that I have heard many pray for his anointing. I mean, why not? After all, people were healed just by Peter's shadow. This sounds and looks attractive, but did Peter not deny Jesus three times? Yes, he was forgiven and went on to becoming a great minister of the Gospel. You want his anointing, but do you want the suffering that he suffered for the Gospel? Do you want his death as well? He was crucified upside down. Is that what you want? What about Apostle Paul, one of the greatest apostles? Did you not read about some of his pain and suffering for the preaching of the Gospel? It was not easy. His anointing came with a great price. *"Are they ministers of Christ? (I speak as a fool) I am more; in labours more abundant, in stripes above measure, in prisons more frequent, in deaths oft. Of the Jews five times received I forty stripes save one. Thrice was I beaten with rods, once was I stoned, thrice I suffered shipwreck, a night and a day I have been in the deep; In journeyings often, in perils of waters, in perils of robbers, in perils by mine own countrymen, in perils by the heathen, in perils in the city, in perils in the wilderness, in perils in the sea, in perils among false brethren; In weariness and painfulness, in watchings often, in hunger and thirst, in fastings often, in cold and nakedness. Beside those things that are without, that which cometh upon me daily, the care of all the churches. Who is weak, and I am not weak? who is offended, and I burn not? If I must needs glory, I will glory of the things which concern mine infirmities" (II Cor. 11:23-30).*

Furthermore, why have a go-between when you have Jesus the Son of God directly giving you His power and authority, knowing that He is always with you to perform that which He has purposed in your life?

Jesus said to ask the Father in His name and the Father would give to us all things. *"And in that day you will ask Me nothing. Most assuredly, I say to you, whatever you ask the Father in My name He will give you" (John 16:23 KJV).* Receiving Peter, Paul, or someone else's mantle is like choosing the secondhand mantle instead of the brand-new mantle tailored to fit you to perfection. Your anointing and your mantle look good on you. They do not look good on anyone else, like theirs would not look good on you. Imagine a four-feet six-inches woman wearing a five-feet eight-inch woman's evening gown. Can you picture it? It doesn't fit, and she probably cannot move in it, and she would look ridiculous in it. Why try to be someone you are not? Why settle for the counterfeit when you have been provided with the authentic? For your sake, do not settle for the false. Having you heard people talking and preaching like other ministers? It is okay to admire an anointed man or woman of God, but don't emulate them; and please do not worship them. You must not have any gods before your Heavenly Father. Remember, He is a jealous God; therefore, do not provoke

Him to anger by mimicking other ministers. Receive the mantle that has been personalized for you by the tailor of heaven Himself. Take your bath. That is, the bath in the blood of Jesus; let it cleanse you and make you pure and holy, ready for the mantle your heavenly Father prepared for you before the foundation of the earth.

The men in the Old Testament and New Testament wore mantles that were personalized for them, according to their office and ministry. You, too, must wear the mantle that is suited for you and your ministry. The Lord gives you His mantle; He suits you up according to His plan and purpose in your life. Not all are apostles and prophets. Not all are teachers and pastors, but all are called according to His purpose. *"Are all apostles? are all prophets? are all teachers? are all workers of miracles? Have all the gifts of healing? do all speak with tongues? do all interpret?" (I Cor. 12:29-30 KJV)*

Know your calling and your ministry so you will know how perfectly fitted is your individualized mantle. It does not matter what your calling is. We are pieces of the puzzle of God, and He has ordained for us to do a work that fits in His plan and eternal purpose. You fit as long as you are in the plan of God, and your part, whatever it is, is vitally important in kingdom work. There is no big me and little you. You are just as important, no matter your calling-the mantle of Jesus is yours; it just might work a little different in you because of your calling and purpose according to the Father's plan for you. Don't you want the mantle that God ordained for you that when people touch you, they are blessed even as the woman with the issue of blood was blessed by just touching the hem of the mantle of Jesus?

This woman had been sick for twelve years, and she had exhausted all her resources to no avail. Imagine living in those days, isolated from everyone because she was considered unclean. Everything and everyone she came in contact became unclean; therefore, she lived in isolation for twelve long years. We have seen what has happened during the coronavirus disease (COVID-19); how people have done unspeakable things because they had to be quarantined in their houses. Imagine twelve years. What would you have done? She desperately needed deliverance. This is why it is so indispensably important for you and me to wear the mantle that has been prepared for us. We must do the work of the Father with excellence. There are many, even today, who need your mantle operating in you strongly. There is a dying world out there, and we must bring Jesus to them powerfully. *"And a certain woman, which had an issue of blood twelve years, And had suffered many things of many physicians, and had spent all that she had, and was nothing bettered, but rather grew worse, When she had heard of Jesus, came in the press behind, and touched his garment. For she said, If I may touch but his clothes, I shall be whole. And straightway the fountain of her blood was dried up; and she felt in her body that she was healed of that plague. And Jesus, immediately knowing in himself that virtue had gone out of him, turned him about in the press, and said, Who touched my clothes? And his disciples said unto him, Thou seest the multitude thronging thee, and sayest thou, Who touched me? And he looked round about to see her that had done this thing. But the woman fearing and trembling, knowing what was done in her, came and fell down before him, and told him all the truth. And he said unto her, Daughter, thy faith hath made thee whole; go in peace, and be whole of thy plague"* (Mk. 5:25-34 KJV). Therefore, put on the mantle of Jesus with the assurance that He, Jesus through His Holy Spirit, is and will be with you to the uttermost parts of the world to perform The Father's heart's desire in you and through you.

Reflection
Tailored Mantle

1. Define tailored mantle.

Chapter 20

Ministering with Authority and with Power

The Father says to you, today, this is the mantle of His heart. He did not ordain any other mantle for you, but the mantle of His one and only begotten and beloved Son, Jesus Christ. The mantle is yours, so exercise the authority and use its power to save the lost, heal the sick, cleanse the lepers, set captives free, raise the dead, and bring your brothers and sisters home. Jesus wants us to leave the ninety-nine who are freed and go get the ones who are in bondage by Satan. *"What man of you, having a hundred sheep, if he loses one of them, does not leave the ninety-nine in the wilderness, and go after the one which is lost until he finds it"* (Luke 15:4 KJV)? We bring them back home to Jesus and we take all the enemy has stolen from us. It is rightfully yours because of the bloodshed of Jesus Christ. Know that if He did not hold Jesus back and gave Him up for you, He will not withhold any good thing from you. He is the benevolent Father. Therefore, to have results before, during, and after, you must pray with confidence and faith in the authority Jesus passed down to you. In other words, you must minister like Jesus did, boldly. After all, it is His anointing power, His authority in His mantle that is in operation; consequently, there is no room for neither doubt nor unbelief. Jesus is the One who is performing the miracles through you and with Him; there is no failure. He always does what is best for His beloved Bride. He is generous and He is kind. He never looks to do you harm. Jesus is always your keeper and your protector. He is the One who gives you what you need, not only to survive, but to live a more abundant life. That is what He died for so you can live in eternal life presently. He has purchased everything you will ever need. All you must do is listen to Jesus attentively, and you will have it all. It is that simple. Do not make it neither harder nor more complicated than what it is. Jesus' will for your life is very clear. He came to seek and save the lost. He came to give you the more abundant life, and He commanded you to go and do the same for others. You must have a purpose with the anointing power of the Holy Spirit. Just as purpose without the resurrection power of the Holy Spirit is useless, so is the power without purpose. Know that God's priority is saving souls. All other ministries are secondary to salvation.

The Father, the One who holds the wind in His fists, who restrains the waters in a garment, and established all the ends of the earth, and who ascended and descended up into heaven, *"Who hath ascended up into heaven, or descended? who hath gathered the wind in his fists? who hath bound the waters in a garment? who hath established all the ends of the earth? what is his name, and what is his son's name, if thou canst tell?" (Prov. 30:4 KJV)* Says to you, "Today, I have equipped you with everything you will ever need to fulfill My calling in your life. I have given you the Name above all names, the name of my Son, Jesus Christ. I have given you the blood of My Son, Jesus Christ. I have given you my precious Holy Spirit with all His powers, gifts, and fruit. I have given you My written Word, the Bible. I have made available legions of angels to minister alongside with you; therefore, all you must do is align yourself with my power and purpose, and you shall be victorious for all is provided in the authority of the mantle of my beloved

Son, Jesus Christ. You lack in no area. You are fully equipped with the armor of God, and you have the intercessor, Jesus Christ, and the intercessor, Holy Spirit, who know what is going on here in earth and in heaven at all times. Therefore, go and conquer in the name of the Father, the Son, and the Holy Spirit." *This dying generation must see signs and wonders following the preaching of the Word. For so long, we have heard dry sermons or even dead sermons. Stale bread is what I call them. Nothing happens after preaching, and we wonder why. Well, some of us have lost our first love, and we are in desperate need of revival. We've got to be revived. Lord, help us! Many unbelievers believe they are doing better than we are, then why become saved, they say? Well, it is not about the here and now entirely. It is about eternal life as well, and without salvation, none will inherit the kingdom of God. That is why we must be revived and preach the Gospel with the power it already possesses in the mantle. Jesus never changes "Jesus Christ the same yesterday, and today, and for ever" (Heb. 13:8 KJV). Therefore, we must change.*

We must use the mantle, and if we need, let us cry to God for revival. We must let go of the things of the past that are holding us planted in the same position. We must allow the Holy Spirit to minister to us in areas that we have blocked or areas, that at times, we have not been willing to let go. We have got to forgive and move on with the Holy Spirit. How will we ever reach our goals or finishing line if we do not put down the heavy loads, we have been carrying for so long? These things keep us staggering. And how will we move on if we are comfortable in yesterday's anointing, doing the same old thing the same old way? Receive the mantle. We allow the choirs to entertain us, the "worship team" to lead us nowhere in worship, and the uninspiring messages, where we shout amen to things that are unscriptural because our flesh is so excited that it does not allow our spirit to discern what is being said. We no longer reverence the house of God; we allow false prophets to teach us, and our gossip has replaced the gospel of Jesus Christ. Yes, you may think I sound harsh, but look around and tell me that we do not need revival. Let's put an end to Satan's schemes, and let's move in the authority of the mantle of Jesus Christ through the resurrection power of His Holy Spirit. The baptism with the Holy Spirit and fire or a new infill with the Holy Spirit is what we desperately need to burn all the impurities of our lives. Let's pray and believe that Jesus will forgive us for our sins and restore unto us His anointing in the authority of His mantle because through the mantle, we have the power to repent and to resist the spirit of fornication and idol worship. We can resist the spirit of Jezebel that is running rampant in some of our churches. *"Notwithstanding I have a few things against thee, because thou sufferest that woman Jezebel, which calleth herself a prophetess, to teach and to seduce my servants to commit fornication, and to eat things sacrificed unto idols" (Rev. 2:20 KJV).* You have the mantle to overcome the second death. *"He that hath an ear, let him hear what the Spirit saith unto the churches; He that overcometh shall not be hurt of the second death" (Rev. 2:11 KJV), and to receive the crown of life. "Fear none of those things which thou shalt suffer: behold, the devil shall cast some of you into prison, that ye may be tried; and ye shall have tribulation ten days: be thou faithful unto death, and I will give thee a crown of life" (Rev. 2:10 KJV).*

Therefore, I say even as King David said, whatever you do, Lord, don't take your Holy Spirit from me. Holy Spirit, help me to live under the authority of the mantle of My Father's heart, daily, and let the fire of God's Word consume me and be shut up in my bones and burn like never before in my heart, causing me to speak out and pray the Word of God and His will for my life and that of the Bride of Christ. Let not your fire be quenched until I am obedient like Jeremiah and King David. *"Then I said, I will not make mention of him, nor speak any more in his name. But his word was in mine heart as a burning fire shut up in my bones, and I was weary with forbearing, and I could not stay. For I heard the defaming of many, fear on every side. The report, say they, and we will report it. All my familiars watched for my halting, saying, Peradventure he will be enticed, and we shall prevail against him, and we shall take our revenge on him" (Jer. 20:9-10 KJV).* "My heart was hot within me, while I was musing the fire burned: then spake I with my tongue, Lord, make me to know mine end, and the measure of my days, what it is: that I may know how frail I am" *(Ps. 39:3 KJV).*

Reflection
Ministering with Authority and with Power

1. How must we pray? Explain.
2. How has the Father equipped you?
3. What is one experience that we are in desperate need from our God, and why?
4. Explain why power must be coupled with purpose.
5. What is your best takeaway from this chapter? Explain.

Conclusion

M any mantles are endeavoring to rest upon you; subsequently, discernment is undeniably necessary to identify, to accept, and to receive the mantle the Father purposely designed for you from the beginning of times. Therefore, you must use wisdom in your choosing.

We have examined some attributes of our Father God. In it, we have discovered, or we have reinforced our knowledge of His character. We know that our God cannot lie, He cannot change, and He cannot break a promise. We see this clearly in the story of Balaam and Balak. Our God's Word cannot be null, nor can it be void. Balak wanted to curse God's people, but God had already blessed them, and because of His unchanging character, Balak's evil end was otiose.

God is omniscient. He knows the end from the beginning. Therefore, those He blesses cannot be cursed. God's Word cannot be destroyed because Jesus is the Word of God, and Jesus and God the Father and God the Holy Spirit are One, loving God.

God is love, and because of His agape love, which is the greatest and the purest love of all, we are not consumed; however, He cannot tolerate sin. Therefore, His love draws us to Him. And we can come to Him with repentant hearts. He will not turn His back on us because He will never hate a broken and contrite heart. He will forgive us and cleanse us from all unrighteousness with the mighty blood of His Son, Jesus Christ, and cause us to be in right standing with Him. His desire is for us to walk in freedom and liberty, and to go with confidence in His love, and in the authority given to us for us to be free and set others free from the grips of the enemy.

The Word of God is true and truth, and we can bank on it because of God's flawless character. We can operate in the authority of the mantle of Jesus with love and with boldness. We do not have to worry about others' negative opinions. We just pray that their eyes and ears are opened to the Spirit of the Living God and the move of God. We understand that Jesus did not leave us comfortless. He sent His precious Holy Spirit to lead and guide us in all truth. He is our teacher and counselor, and He is the Spirit of our all-wise God. He never leads us astray. He loves us too much for that, and we know the love of the Father, through His Son, Jesus Christ's sacrifice. Therefore, let's walk with our Heavenly Father, allowing no satanic distractions. We must stay focused and on track with our Father's will for our lives, with the teaching and preaching of the Good News, so that many can come home. Let's present many to Jesus because salvation makes Jesus happy. I cannot, nor do I want to forget the vision Jesus gave me recently about the multitude coming to Him for salvation. Jesus was so pleased. Again, salvation makes Jesus happy. After all, that is why He shed His blood and gave His life. We must keep focused and be about our Father's heart, always. We cannot afford the luxury of ungodly alliances.

It behooves us to carefully align ourselves with God's chosen leaders in ministry. The mantle of the Father's heart is the only true mantle; all others are false. We do not live in the Old Testament. Hence, there is no need to look for another's mantle. The mantle of Jesus gives you the authority to overcome obstacles, to live, and to receive the rewards purchased for you by the blood of the Lamb of God, Jesus Christ. The mantle is yours. Use the weapons the

Lord has given you under the authority in the mantle of Jesus, His beloved, to live in the more abundant life-the overflow of the Father's heart right now. Your pure and holy worship opens the door to the Lord's presence, which is where you want to be, always. You enter in, seeking His heart and face, and not His hands. Here is where you can sit and relax with the faith of a child on your Daddy's lap as you lean in His bosom while listening to His heartbeat. Here, the false cannot enter. You have access to the Father's heart and the mantle of His heart because He loves you and gave His Son Jesus Christ for you. If He did not keep Jesus from you, His pride and joy, He will not keep anything else from you. Go, therefore, in the love of the Father and conquer for His glory. The authority in the mantle of the Father's heart is yours.

Live it!

Don't mind if I take a moment here to talk directly to Jesus. I just have to tell Him that I LOVE HIM. "Lord Jesus, you are my Jesus, and I love you very much. My sweet Heavenly Lord Jesus, I thank you for praying for us, and for restoring the glory that was stolen from us by Satan back in the Garden of Eden." *"And he said, I heard thy voice in the garden, and I was afraid, because I was naked; and I hid myself." (Gen. 3:10 KJV).* We were at one time clothed with the glory of God, but sin caused us to become naked and ashamed before our Father. We inherited from Adam the stripping of the glory of God after he and Eve fell for the tricks of the enemy. *"For all have sinned, and come short of the glory of God" (Rom. 3:23 KJV).* But now, Jesus has restored all things to us, including the glory of His Father God. He has equipped His Bride by giving us His glory, the glory of the Father's heart. "Jesus, you have given unto us the glory that the Father gave you so the world may know and believe that the Father has sent you, and you have sent us, for we are one in one accord with the Father, with the Son, and with the Holy Spirit. We are your Body, who is connected to your Head, Jesus Christ. We, your precious Bride, move in tune with you, and we go in the power of the authority in your mantle, the mantle of the Father's heart, to make the world know and believe that you came, and you are coming again, soon."

"Neither pray I for these alone, but for them also which shall believe on me through their word; That they all may be one; as thou, Father, art in me, and I in thee, that they also may be one in us: that the world may believe that thou hast sent me. And the glory which thou gavest me I have given them; that they may be one, even as we are one: I in them, and thou in me, that they may be made perfect in one; and that the world may know that thou hast sent me, and hast loved them, as thou hast loved me" (John 17:20-23 KJV).

Reflection Questions

The Mantle of the Father's Heart–It's Your Mantle

True or False: Are the following statements *true* or *false*? If the Scripture is incorrect, identify the correct Scripture.

1. _____   According to Matthew 6:3, God cannot lie.
2. _____   John 3:2 says that God cannot change.
3. _____   According to Hebrews 6:18, it is impossible for God to lie.
4. _____   Proverbs 22:18 says that he who finds a wife finds a good thing and is blessed of the Lord.
5. _____   According to Hebrews 13:8, Jesus is the same forever.
6. _____   God cannot break His promise according to Eccl. 5:5.
7. _____   According to Revelation 1:4, God is the Alpha and Omega, the beginning and the ending...
8. _____   Luke 11:13 declares that God gives of the Holy Spirit to them who ask of Him.
9. _____   "Heaven and earth shall pass away, but my words shall not pass away." Matt 24:35
10. _____   According to Mark 16:10, "...the Lord working with them and confirming the word with sings following. Amen."

Multiple Choice: Select the correct answer.

1. "Every good gift and every perfect gift is from above, and cometh down from the Father of Lights with whom is not variableness, neither shadow of turning."
    A. James 1:17
    B. Matthew 6:2
    C. Job 3:1
    D. It is not really known

2. "Arise, shine; for thine light is come, and he glory of the Lord is risen upon thee."
    A. Matthew 6:2
    B. Job 3:1
    C. Isaiah 60:1
    D. James 1:17

3. "Thy kingdom come, Thy will be done in earth, as it is in heaven."
    A. Job 3:1
    B. Matthew 6:10
    C. James 1:17
    D. Matthew 6:2

4. "And take the helmet of salvation, and the sword of the Spirit, which is the word of God."
    A. Matthew 6:10
    B. James 1:17
    C. Matthew 6:2
    D. Ephesians 6:17

5. "For the word of God is quick, and powerful and sharper than any two-edged sword, piercing even to the dividing asunder of soul and spirit, and of the joints and marrow, and is a discerner of the thoughts and intents of the heart."
   A. Matthew 6:2
   B. Ephesians 6:17
   C. James 1:17
   D. Hebrews 4:12

6. "And it is easier for heaven and earth to pass, than one tittle of the law to fail."
   A. Ephesians 6:17
   B. Matthew 6:2
   C. James 1:17
   D. Luke 16:17

7. "Pride goes before destruction and a haughty spirit before a fall."
   A. Romans 8:36
   B. Ruth 1:16
   C. Proverbs 16:18
   D. John 14:6

9. "Do we then make void the law through faith? God forbid: yea, we establish the law."
   A. Romans 3:31
   B. Hebrews 13:8
   C. Matthew 5:17
   D. Romans 8:36

10. "For the life of the flesh is in the blood: and I have given it to you upon the altar to make atonement for your souls: for it is the blood that maketh an atonement for the soul."

A. Exodus 1:3

B. Genesis 3:15

C. Leviticus 17:11

D. II Chronicles 7:14

Select the correct answer.

A. Job	B. Sisera	C. Adversaries	D. Saul

1. _____   The mantle of death
2. _____   The mantle of confusion
3. _____   The mantle of judgment
4. _____   The mantle of worship, mourning, and repentance

A. Elisha	B. Jonadab	C. Daughter of Israel	D. Eros

5. _____   Son of Rechab
6. _____   Transferring of mantle
7. _____   The mantle removal
8. _____   Spirit of lust

Paragraph: In short paragraphs, answer the following:

1. How is Jesus' blood incorruptible?
2. Define living in the overflow.
3. Define *shalom*.
4. Explain the death of Nadab and Abihu.
5. Describe repentance.
6. Tell the difference between authority and power.
7. Define the word *mantle*.
8. Describe the mantle of the Father's heart.
9. Define agape love.
10. Define dew of God.
11. Explain why it is wrong to covet someone else's anointing.
12. Have you ever felt that you were not whole? Explain.
13. How has your relationship with God deepened from the reading of this book?
14. Is the mantle of the Father's heart for you, why or why not? Support your answer with at least three Scriptures.

Prayers

Prayer to Break Soul Ties

Dear Heavenly Father,
I humbly come to you in the precious name of your Son, Jesus Christ.

Heavenly Father, I come boldly to the Throne of Grace, covered in the precious and mighty blood of Jesus. Lord, I know that you always hear my prayers, and You answer each and every one of them because I pray for the desires of your heart.

Heavenly Father, today, I am asking for your Holy Spirit, the all-seeing eyes, the seven Spirits of God, to take me back as I am covered in the precious blood of Jesus, to all the places and people that I left a piece of my soul behind willingly and or unwillingly due to my ignorance and even disobedience. First of all, Father, I pray that you forgive me for my involvement in scattering pieces of my soul. I am truly sorry, and I repent of my evil doings. Heavenly Father, thank you for forgiving me even as I forgive all those involved in my past, whether their involvements were spiritual, physical, mental, emotional, financial or in all of those areas. Lord, I forgive them and put them in your hands so they, too, can be set free and live in the freedom and liberty that is found in your Son, Jesus. Now, Lord, I ask the Holy Spirit to collect every scattered piece in Jesus' name, and bring them together and make me whole. Father, In the powerful name of Jesus, pluck up all the thorny roots of ungodly seeds planted in my life; I break all the ungodly spiritual, verbal, emotional, physical, mental, and financial alliances with every person I have ever been connected to, and to all those that they were connected to before, during, and after our relationship, up until right now because, Lord, before I broke the ties with them, all that they were adding to their bank of despair were added to me as well. Heavenly Father, I break the cords of bondage, and I burn them into ashes and scatter them, so they are never put together again against me and my loved ones. Holy Spirit, thank you for leading me in my deliverance. Thank you that I have been set free and made whole in the name of Jesus. Father, I seal this prayer with the blood of Jesus, the resurrection power of the Holy Spirit, and the love of God in Jesus' name. Amen!

THE MANTLE OF THE FATHER'S HEART PRAYER

Lord Jesus,

Thank you for equipping me with the mantle filled with your authority that is backed by the Ancient of Days, and backed up by the omnipotent, omniscient, benevolent, and eternal God. Let it rest upon my life with your power, love, compassion, and mercy.

Heavenly Father,

I strip myself naked from all other mantles. I renounce all counterfeit and illegal mantles. I rebuke them in the name and blood of your precious Son, Jesus Christ, and I make myself bathe in the blood of Jesus for purification, righteousness, and readiness for your glorified mantle to operate in my life like never before.

Precious Holy Spirit,

Give me an accelerated understanding of the supernatural power of the mantle of the Father's heart, so I, a Word carrier, may move expeditiously in tune with you to perform the Father's heart here on earth. I want to please the Father, the Son, and the Holy Spirit. Refill my spirit with your presence, with your love, and with your fire for your glory, Lord. Amen!

THE OVERFLOW PRAYER

Dear Heavenly Father,

I humbly bow down before your Throne of Grace in the name of your precious Son, Jesus the Christ. Father, I pray as you look at me that you see the blood sacrifice of your Son. Jesus, I thank you for your blood, for it gives me direct access to my Heavenly Father's presence without fear, but with clean, uplifted hands and a reverent heart. Holy Spirit, thank you for the vision of the overflow. I thank you, Father, that you are generous with your children, and you are extravagant in your giving. Father, if you did not spare Jesus, your most extravagant gift, but gave Him up for me, and Jesus, if you did not keep your life from me, you will not withhold any good thing from me either. Father, I receive of the overflow of your heart and of the overflow of your love; I receive of the overflow of your mercy and of the overflow of your compassion. Heavenly Father, you gave me the vision of the overflow. You gave the dream of your dew. Father, I trust in your communication with me, because, Jesus, you said that your sheep know your voice. I trust in your Word, because Father, you are the God who cannot lie, who cannot change, and you do not go back on your promises. Thank you for the vision of the open heaven and the vision of the falling precious stone falling from heaven. Lord, I lift all these visions and dreams to you right now, knowing that you are the promise keeper. You are my shepherd, and I shall not be in want. I thank you, Heavenly Father, that I live in the abundance of your overflow, because Lord, all my needs have been met, and my wants do not exist. I am completely satisfied in your presence, and I desire to dwell in your presence more than anything else in this Word. Father, I know and understand that my financial overflow is to further the gospel of Jesus Christ, my master. Thank you for trusting me with your resources. Amazing Holy Spirit, thank you for opening my spiritual eyes to see all the blessings that were provided for me on the Cross of Calvary by my Lord and Savior, Jesus Christ. Holy Spirit, thank you for opening my ears to hear the instruction of the Father concerning my resources. Father, I love you and honor you with all your gifts to me. Holy Spirit, give me your gift of generosity, so I may give liberally to the poor, the widow, and strongly support the preaching of the Good News. Father, again, I thank you for being the great Daddy that you are to your children. Lord, in the abundance of your love, I collect all of my past prayers, not only for financial blessings, but most importantly for the abundance of souls saved, healed, delivered, and discipled for your glory and honor. Lord, I seal this prayer in the name of the Father, the Son, and the Holy Spirit. Holy Spirit, seal it with your wall of fire of protection, for your abundance is worthy of protection, in Jesus' name. Amen!

THE MANTLE OF THE FATHER'S HEART PRAYER FOR THE BELIEVER

Dear Heavenly Father,

I join your Son, Jesus Christ, and your precious Holy Spirit right now in intercession for the readers of this book. Heavenly Father, I know that you have spoken to their hearts while they read it. I know, Father, that their spiritual eyes have been opened wider because of your love for them. You have spoken by your Holy Spirit, and you have reached to the deepest depth of their hearts, and you have spoken forcefully, yet, softly and gently into their lives. Father, you are merciful and compassionate. Your compassion moves in their hearts even as they read this prayer originated in your heart. Your children are blessed because you have blessed them mightily. Thank you, Father, your love, mercy, and compassion are so sweet. They are fresh and new every morning. Thank you, Lord Jesus, that they see the benefits of the authority in your mantle, operating in them for your glory. Father, I release legions of ministering angels to work on their behalf and mine right now and always. Angels, I agree with the Father on your assignments concerning God's people. Go and perform them in Jesus' name and for Jesus' glory. Thank you, Father, that your children see and experience the authority of Jesus moving in them and through them, even now. Thank you, Lord Jesus! I seal this prayer in the love of the Father, the sacrifice of Jesus' blood, and the resurrection power of the Holy Spirit, in Jesus' name. Amen!

Author's Biography

D r. Benedita Monteiro Gomes is the daughter of João Nepomuceno Gomes and Zuilda Monteiro Gomes. She was born on the island of São Nicolau, Cabo-Verde, West Coast of Africa. She is the mother of three beautiful children- Bonny, Christopher and Bobbie, and she is a grandmother to five amazing grandchildren-Jackson, Cazmire, Vida, Christiana and Saintil. She is an ordained-pastor, a Spanish/English teacher, adjunct-professor, and a polyglot. She is the Dorchester County Public Schools 2018-2019 Teacher of the Year, the author of the Voice in the Cup and founder of Resurrection Power Ministries III.

Dr. Benedita Monteiro Gomes has traveled to over thirty countries to teach, preach and intercede for the nations. She is devoted to spreading the Gospel of Jesus Christ. She earned her Doctorate Degree in Biblical Studies from New Life Bible College and Seminary: her M. A. in Teaching English to Students of Other Languages (TESOL) from Salisbury University, a B.A. in Spanish from Delaware State University and her Associate's Degree in Computer Accounting from Yorktown Business Institute.